T0315703

# WALKS THROUGH HISTORY
# IPSWICH

# WALKS THROUGH HISTORY
# IPSWICH

## CAROL TWINCH

DB
PUBLISHING

First published in Great Britain in 2011 by The Derby Books Publishing Company Limited, 3 The Parker Centre, Derby, DE21 4SZ.

This paperback edition published in Great Britain in 2013 by DB Publishing, an imprint of JMD Media Ltd

ISBN 978-1-78091-322-3

Printed and bound in the UK by Copytech (UK) Ltd Peterborough

# Contents

# INTRODUCTION

The ancient town of Ipswich sits astride the River Orwell at what was once a shallow point in its course, fordable between the two banks, near to the present-day Stoke Bridge. Although archaeology is able to pinpoint early revetments associated with the crossing, it is unwise to be too precise when it comes to where rivers were flowing before the 6th century, or what they were called by those who knew them. Traditionally the name *Gipping*, or *Gyp*, combined with *wic* (a port or settlement beside a river), led to *Gipeswic* in various forms, then *Yppyswyche* and finally Ipswich. Further investigation suggests that (a) the *Gip(e)* or *Gippa* refers to a Saxon chief whose *wic* (village or small town) it was or (b) a *Gip* referred to the bend on the river on which the village stands. What is known, however, is that by the 10th century the town now known as Ipswich was called *Gipeswic*, we are certain about this as it appears on coins minted in the reign of King Edgar.

The river crossing was already well-established by the time of the Norman Conquest. The church of St Mary at Stoke appears in the 1086 *Domesday Book* but recent archaeology proves that a significant trading settlement existed at least as early as the 6th century. Ipswich is now held to be one of the oldest towns in England to have been continuously inhabited since that time.

When the Romans left in AD410 the hiatus was filled by Angles, Saxons and Jutes so that by AD550 three separate communities had established themselves at the Stoke crossing (*Gipeswic*), Boss Hall and Handford. Halfway through the 7th century, Boss Hall and Handford were abandoned but *Gipeswic* grew and flourished. Thus it was the Early Anglo-Saxons who developed the port and laid the foundations for urban expansion and permanence.

So why, then, is there so little visual evidence of this antiquity? Certainly, Ipswich deserves its reputation as a town of change, and it did so because prosperity at various times in its history afforded the opportunity to demolish and rebuild. This accounts for the relative lack of visual signs of the five religious houses that were in the town until the Reformation. Those at the helm took on the challenges of change and were never afraid to embrace modernity. The town needed to keep pace with constantly fluctuating economic circumstances and today is no different; it is still evolving. There seem to be constant building and renovation works that spring up around the town, only to disappear and re-appear somewhere else.

Town nostalgia books show endless photographic scenes captioned 'this was demolished in the 1930s', or the 1960s, 70s or 80s. Road-widening schemes over the years led to the wholesale removal of historic buildings and such was the dramatic speed and seemingly reckless havoc wrought in the town in the 1960s, the era of progress gone mad, that the Ipswich Society was formed with the aim of preserving the best of the town's old buildings and monitoring future development. The most dramatic alterations taking place in the 21st century are seen on the Waterfront which has been in a state of flux now for some years, although the recession has temporarily slowed things down of late. The University Campus Suffolk buildings (referred to as UCS which also stands for its other appellation of University College Suffolk) dominate the eastern quays. There are currently ambitious plans to develop the Stoke Bridge area, which will again change the face of the Waterfront. If you are absent from Ipswich for even a week there is bound to be change of some description going on, somewhere. At time of writing the words 'Edward Fison Ltd' still appears on a red-brick wall on the Stoke side and, until recently, the London Underground logo adorned a nearby wall (the computerised control system used by London Underground was operated from here). However, development work has already begun on Stoke quay so that part of the Ipswich landscape will be changed by the time this book is published.

*Walks Through History* does not set out to record too much of the unseen history of Ipswich (of which there is a copious supply) but instead offers the chance for the visitor, whether local or from afar, to see what is here today, how it features in the town's history and get a taste of what the town is all about. The archaeologists constantly re-write history and academicians amend and re-shape the way we think about the past. But it is invariably left to the local historian to see how it all fits together with what is left 'on the ground'.

Whether by coincidence or design, the modern town architecture is one of reflection. The UCS building mirrors the masts of the Neptune Marina, the New Suffolk College glows with the available light, the Willis Building illuminates the surrounds from its many angles, while the Wet Dock and River Orwell offer a myriad of calm and rippling reflections of sky, clouds and river craft of many types. Yet in spite of its modern face, the town and port nevertheless have their roots firmly in a long and distinguished past.

Ipswich has a commendable number of sculptures and other art forms scattered around the town. Some are mentioned as each walk progresses but there are many more to be enjoyed. One or two walks overlap but that is unavoidable and, where appropriate, they are cross-referenced.

Some of the churches are open every day, such as St Mary le Tower and St Mary at Elms, but others (especially those redundant) are only open at certain times (or give details of a key holder on the church notice board). Further information is available on the Ipswich Borough Council website or from the

Tourist Information Centre (referred to as the TIC throughout). Details can be found in Useful Information and Contacts at the back of this book. Many churches have guide books which contain more information than can be included here. Most are written or inspired by Roy Tricker, whose knowledge of Ipswich churches is second to none.

Ipswich has been the county town of Suffolk since 1974 and like any such town it has a good number of cafés and restaurants, as well as resting places in shady nooks, especially in the several churchyards. It is advisable to take advantage of these to read through the walks before starting out as it is not easy trying to read standing beside a busy road. There are benches in and around the TIC in Arras Square and in summertime the town embraces café society. Tables and chairs are to be found in St Lawrence's churchyard, St Nicholas Centre, Christchurch Park, Curson Plain, Pal's Bar and along the Waterfront.

All walks make use of pedestrian crossings where possible. There are black-and-white sign posts throughout the town to help guide the way. The sketch maps are not to scale. Town maps are available at the TIC to give an overall view of the town centre.

Although *Walks Through History* takes the form of town walks, it can as easily be read in a comfortable chair, a kind of fireside ramble through just a few of the innumerable strands of Ipswich history. Lately, there has been a noticeably increased interest in town history. The band of town guides is constantly surprised and delighted by the number of locals who join the visitors on their conducted walks. Invariably is heard 'I've lived here all my life and never noticed that before!'

Many thanks to those who helped in preparing this book, especially the Ipswich Tourist Information Centre staff, Ipswich Town Guides, Keith Bonnick (Cuming Museum, London Borough of Southwark), David Annand, River Gipping Trust, Neil Jones (Trinity House), Simon Meyer (Steeple Keeper, St Mary-le-Bow), Robert and Pearl Simper, and Dr David Jones (Colchester & Ipswich Museum Service).

# TOWN TRANSPORT

Bus and train timetables and routes are liable to change from time to time so it is always worth checking before embarking on a journey.

Information is correct at time of publication.

## PARK AND RIDE
www.suffolkonboard.com
0845 606 6067

Suffolk County Council operates Park and Ride schemes Monday to Saturday every 10 minutes between 7am and 7pm. Ask the driver for the nearest stop for the town centre.

**London Road – Postcode IP8 3TQ**
Situated at Copdock Mill at the interchange off the A12/A14

**Martlesham – Postcode IP5 3QX**
Situated at the roundabout where the A1214 meets the A12

## TOWN CAR PARKS
Motorists are encouraged to use Park and Ride but the Waterfront and University Campus Suffolk (UCS) car parks are signposted

Information relating to the main town car parks can be found on www.ipswich.gov.uk or www.ncp.co.uk

## IPSWICH TOWN CENTRE CIRCULAR (FREE SHUTTLE BUS) ROUTE 38
Sponsored by Suffolk County Council
Runs every 20 minutes at designated stops but originating in front of Endeavour House in Russell Road
Traveline 0871 200 22 33

## IPSWICH TOWN BUSES
Tower Ramparts
www.ipswichbuses.co.uk
Timetable Enquiries 0800 919390

## FIRST EASTERN COUNTIES BUSES LTD
6 Dogs Head Street
Ipswich, IP4 1AD
01473 253734
County and national buses

## RAILWAY STATION
Burrell Road,
Ipswich, IP2 8AL
**www.nationalexpresseastanglia.com**

## NATIONAL CYCLE NETWORK
Ipswich Waterfront is now on the National Cycle Network Route 51, which means it will soon be possible to cycle from Oxford to Ipswich. Also from Ipswich to Bury St Edmunds on the Goldeneye Suffolk cycle routes.

# THE WESTERN APPROACH

Walk 1 is a circular walk that starts and finishes at Cornhill, taking in:
*Cornhill – Westgate Street – Museum Street – St Mary's Court – High Street – Lady Lane – Chapman Lane – New Wolsey Theatre – Black Horse Lane – Elm Street – St Mary at Elms – Arcade Street – Lion Street – King Street – Giles Circus – Princes Street – Cornhill*

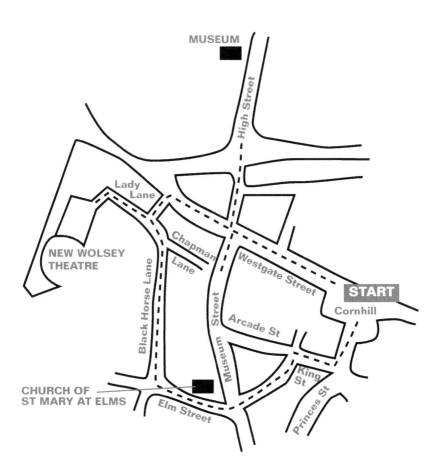

*There is a long tradition of markets on Cornhill, now held in front of the Town Hall.*

This is intended as an exploration of the western section of the main town. There are several cafés and resting places along the way, and nowhere is very far from the town centre.

Cornhill has been the commercial and urban centre of Ipswich since the town's Anglo-Saxon origins. As its name suggests, here was the traditional place for trading corn and of mediaeval markets and fairs. Jugglers, dancers, musicians and itinerant preachers vied for attention as people went about their business amid the hustle and bustle of the street vendors. Itinerant merchants from Europe rubbed shoulders not only with townspeople but also those from the surrounding countryside who brought produce from the farms to sell in the town. Pilgrims and travellers mingled with the stall holders and, from the 12th century until the Reformation, mendicant friars from four orders were an additional and very visible part of the melange of street life.

Markets are still held on Cornhill. Traditionally they were on Tuesdays and Saturdays but they now operate four days a week on Tuesdays, Thursdays, Fridays and Saturdays.

Where the Victorian Town Hall now stands (open to the public and home to the Borough Council's Town Hall Galleries) stood an early mediaeval church dedicated to St Mildred, built around AD700 under the royal patronage of the East Anglian rulers, the Wuffinga kings. It is believed that Ipswich (or *Gipeswic* as it was then called) was the port for the Wuffingas' Great Hall at Rendlesham. Best known of the kings is Raedwald, who died around 625 and is buried at Sutton Hoo on the River Deben a few miles to the north. There would have been an overlord in the town who owed allegiance either to the Wuffingas or some other royal house whose job it was to supervise the trading activities of the port and link up with the rural network inland.

St Mildred's is depicted on the official town seal of 1200 (Walk 2). The church was deconsecrated sometime in the 14th century and adapted for use as the town's earliest Guildhall and seat of local government. Much of the fabric was lost in the reorganisation of Cornhill in 1812 and the last vestige disappeared in the building of the Town Hall in 1867.

Throughout the ages, Cornhill has been continuously a venue for either religious worship or as a place where local government officers and the king's clerks conducted their business. It was the setting for civic functions and assembly, and where law enforcement was meted out.

From Norman times until the late 18th century the pillory was used at Cornhill to punish those fishmongers and butchers who sold tainted food and millers who charged more than the regulated price. Miscreants were placed there by order of the Justices of the Peace. In 1761 one Thomas Herd was stood in the pillory and was 'severely pelted by the populace'.

In 1607 the stocks, an ancient punishment for 'rogues, vagabonds, drunks' and other petty offenders, were moved to Cornhill.

'Whipping at the cart' was carried out here in the 16th century. The prisoner, with naked back, was tied to the back of a cart which was drawn by a horse three times round the Cornhill while being whipped with a cat-o'-nine-tails.

During the persecutions of Queen Mary's reign, Protestants were burnt at the stake for their faith. In 1556, Joan Trunchfield, a shoemaker's wife, and Agnes Potten, a beer-maker's wife, were both burned to death in one fire on Cornhill. The nine Protestant martyrs are named on the Ipswich Martyrs' Memorial in Christchurch Park (Walk 3).

During the 1645 witchcraft trials, Mary 'Mother' Lackland was tried in the Moot Hall (fashioned from the fabric of St Mildred's church) and condemned to death by burning. She was the only 'witch' burnt in England (they were usually hanged) but this was because she was also convicted of killing her husband. Although she was tried on Cornhill, Mother Lackland was likely to have been burned on Rushmere Heath which was the usual place of execution at the time.

Until 1863 hangings were carried out in public, often in the presence of a large crowd – some of which had travelled miles to witness the spectacle. The last public execution was carried out in 1863 when a labourer, John Ducker, was hanged for murder.

A market cross once stood in the middle of Cornhill, erected in about 1628 to replace an earlier cross dating from 1510. In 1723 a town grandee and Ipswich MP, Francis Negus, presented a lead statue then known as *Flora, Goddess of Flowers*, to the town. After being equipped with a sword and scales, Flora was placed on top of the market cross to serve as *Astrea, Goddess of Justice*. There she remained until 1812 when the cross was demolished during the improvements made to Cornhill. Thrifty councillors, however, kept the statue and replaced the sword and scales with a sickle and wheat sheaf. Her new role was as *Ceres, Goddess of Agriculture* and she was placed on top of the new Corn Exchange. When this was demolished to make way for the (Old) Post Office, she was for a while in Christchurch Mansion before eventually finding her way to the foot of the main staircase in the Town Hall, where she can be seen today.

In the 18th and early 19th century the market cross became a favourite meeting place for the military personnel from the town's barracks, who added colour and glamour to the town's street scene.

In the south-east corner stands the Old Post Office, built on the site of the first Corn Exchange in 1881 which in turn had replaced the Georgian Rotunda, the town's first shopping centre. Prior to that, it had been the site of the shambles (or butchery). Here would have stood the bull stake (or ring) used for bull baiting. The Corporation would not allow beef to be sold unless

*Cornhill is still used for ceremonial occasions.*

it had previously been tortured, or baited, by dogs. In the reign of Edward IV it was ordered that butchers be fined if they were found to be selling unbaited bull's flesh.

During the reign of Elizabeth I, a fine of one shilling was imposed on butchers who offered for sale the flesh of a bull that had not been baited for an hour on the day on which it was sold.

The practice was abolished in 1676 and the bull ring broken up.

*Crew of HMS* Quorn *approach Cornhill to receive the Freedom of Ipswich.*

*The Band of the Royal Marines in front of the Old Post Office in the corner of Cornhill.*

The Corn Exchange moved to King Street (to the south of the Town Hall), where it remained until finally closed in the 1970s. It re-opened in 1975 as an entertainment and arts centre.

As well as the weekly markets on Cornhill, civic ceremonies also take place in front of the Town Hall, usually presided over by the Town Mayor. Under the Municipal Corporations Act of 1835 the borough was thereafter possessed of a mayor, 10 aldermen and 30 councillors. The mayor is 'made' at the Annual General Meeting of the Council.

Mannings in the south-west corner is the oldest surviving building on Cornhill. Next door is the Golden Lion, where the coaches *Telegraph* and *Volunteer* stopped to change horses on the way to Yarmouth.

**Leave Cornhill and proceed along Westgate Street.**

Composed today chiefly of retail outlets, Westgate Street once contained many inns and was the main route into town for travellers from London and Norwich who entered via the West Gate (sometimes called St Matthew's Gate) at the far end of the street.

In the coaching era of the 18th and 19th centuries, passengers were picked up from the Crown and Anchor (now WH Smith) and dropped off at the old Suffolk Hotel which stood on the opposite site of the road. There were daily coach services from Norwich, Yarmouth and London.

*The old Crown & Anchor Hotel building on Westgate Street, now WH Smith.*

**A little further down on the left-hand side is Museum Street.**

A short way down Museum Street on the left is Arlingtons café-bar & brassiere, which was the original museum. It takes its name from when it was called Arlingtons Ballroom.

The building was commissioned as the town's first museum in 1846 and opened the following year 'to educate the working classes in natural history'. It gained national repute under the Revd Professor John Stevens Henslow who had been Charles Darwin's mentor at Cambridge University and was one of the vice-presidents (and later president). It was supported by the leading bankers, brewers and public spirited families of the day – Cobbold, Alexander, Ransome and Tollemache.

The staircase at Arlingtons was saved by the architect Christopher Fleury from Thomas Seckford's Great Place (see below), which was demolished to make way for the museum.

Initially, general admission was for subscribers only, but there was free entry on certain evenings when a committee member 'explained objects' to the duly-assembled 'working class'. Insufficient income from subscribers led to the Corporation taking it over in 1853 and increasing free opening times. Dr William Barnard Clarke (son of a senior portman) was appointed curator and an attendant employed to prevent 'the idle and dissolute' from entering.

*The original Town Museum, now Arlingtons, on Museum Street.*

*The Elizabethan staircase at Arlingtons was saved from Thomas Seckford's Great Place.*

The attendant was not entirely successful, it seems, as Dr Clarke complained about the 'vile and disorderly mob that contaminates our rooms on public nights'. The public, he said, was 'dirty, smelly and noisy' and its members rushed up and down stairs howling and shrieking. Such meetings, he thought, were excuses for immoral purposes. They also left piles of peanut shells behind, peanuts being the prevailing snack of the day and invariably used as missiles by theatre-goers to register their disapproval of a particular performance.

In 1881 it was decided that the Corporation would build its own premises in High Street to house the museum, library and science and art schools. The new museum opened in 1881 with galleries for natural history, archaeology, ethnography and geology. The old museum then had a variety of uses thereafter including, in the 1960s, as ballroom which was said to be haunted by a boa constrictor donated to the old museum in its early days.

There is a small display concerning the museum on the first floor in Arlingtons.

Opposite Arlingtons is the Museum Street Methodist Church. The foundation stone was laid in 1860 and on 27 March 1861 it opened for worship. A minister's house was built at the rear of the building (which can be seen from Black Horse Lane, see below).

To the south of the Methodist chapel is a rare glimpse of Georgian architecture. Very little was built at this time as it was a low period in the

*Museum Street's rare Georgian houses and (right) Methodist chapel.*

Spirit of Youth *in St Mary's Court (just off Museum Street).*

town's fortunes when there were no moneyed gentry or rich merchants anxious to make their mark on the town face.

Heading back towards Westgate Street, on the left-hand side is a small opening into St Mary's Court (at 16A) where can be seen one of the many town sculptures, *Spirit of Youth*, by John Ravera.

*The Victorian Town Museum is now on High Street.*

**Returning to Westgate Street, proceed north onto High Street, crossing at the junction with St Matthews Street and Crown Street.**

High Street is aptly named, not because it is the main thoroughfare, as the town's street plan was laid down long before towns were given High Streets, but because (like Fonnereau Road, Walk 3) it rises steeply away from the town.

Halfway up High Street is Ipswich Museum, built in 1880 with the exhibits moved there the following year from their original home on Museum Street.

Among the current exhibits is found the story of the Roman occupation of Suffolk and comprehensive histories of the archaeology, flora and fauna of the area.

Here is also the story of the town's Anglo-Saxon beginnings (Walk 5) showing a craftsman working antlers of large red deer, brought over from Germany for skilled workers to make combs, and needles for weaving and leather working.

*A museum exhibit of a craftsman working imported antlers.*

The gorillas were the first ever seen in Britain and were shot by Paul Belloni du Chaillu (died 1903), African explorer, anthropologist and author of the children's novel *Stories of the Gorilla Country* (1867) and other Victorian adventure stories. Du Chaillu sold the gorillas to the Ipswich Museum and may well have visited it as he had Suffolk connections. He was great friends with the banker, writer and anthropologist Edward Clodd of Aldeburgh.

Two doors up from the museum is the Ipswich Art School Gallery, which opened in 2010. Exhibitions change every six months and the gallery is open to the public most days.

**Returning to Westgate Street, turn right and continue past Black Horse Walk on the left.**

This is almost the end of Westgate Street and here is where the ancient West Gate stood, which guarded this entrance to the town for over 400 years. The lower section dated from the 12th century and the upper part the 14th century, although it had been partially rebuilt in the 1440s and used as the town gaol. It was demolished in 1781 when the ever-increasing volume of traffic that needed to pass through the narrow entrance made it a bottle neck which threatened the town's commerce.

Large numbers of itinerant traders, pilgrims and visitors would pass through the gate daily, particularly on market days, making it the most important of the town entrances. In summer they would be drawn to one of the many inns and hostelries that lined Westgate Street which also served pilgrims visiting the mediaeval Shrine of Our Lady of Ipswich just outside the West Gate.

**A short way along is a left-hand turning into Lady Lane.**

The size of Lady Lane belies its importance in the town from the 12th to 16th centuries as a place of pilgrimage. The Shrine Chapel of Our Lady of Grace, sometimes called the Chapel of the Ipswich Madonna, was first chronicled in 1152 and attracted pilgrims for around 400 years.

Our Lady had a huge following in the town and there are six mediaeval Marian dedications among the town churches. Although in pre-Reformation times there were 16 shrines to St Mary in Suffolk alone, this was the only one known locally as 'Our Lady of Grace'.

Pilgrims came from near and far to visit the shrine and the feast day of the Assumption of the Blessed Virgin Mary was widely observed in the Middle Ages. Ipswich is one of the oldest centres of Christian pilgrimage in the world

*The* Madonna of Ipswich *statue in Lady Lane, which once led to the Shrine of Our Lady of Grace.*

and its shrine ranked alongside Walsingham (Norfolk) in importance and popularity.

Princess Elizabeth, daughter of Edward I (1272–1307) visited the shrine chapel in 1297 before her marriage to the Count of Holland. Edward escorted his daughter to the town and stayed for a few days 'with a splendid court'. The king's entourage filled the town with the razzmatazz of thousands of London visitors, wedding guests, soldiers, craftsmen, street performers and minstrels, not to mention Dutch troops and the count's own attendants.

Queen Katherine of Aragon and Henry VIII came separately to the shrine, as did Sir Thomas More (1478–1530), who visited on more than one occasion. Cardinal Wolsey (Walk 5) is recorded visiting the chapel in 1517.

Thomas More witnessed a miracle that took place there: a young girl, the daughter of Sir Roger Wentworth, suffered terrible seizures but when she was taken to the chapel and beheld the image of Our Lady she was restored to health 'in the presence of all the company'.

At the Reformation, shrines to Our Lady were dismantled and their images broken or burned. The reformers reacted strongly against what they perceived to be the excessive devotion of the Roman Catholic Church to St Mary. Except where a Lady Chapel was within a church there was seldom any sanctity attached to the building which contained them, thus shrine chapels fell quickly into ruin or were pulled down. The statue of the Madonna and Child that had stood in the Ipswich Chapel since the 12th century was taken to Chelsea in 1538 to be burnt, along with that of Our Lady of Walsingham.

The story goes that the statue was rescued by English sailors who took it on board ship but had to take refuge from a storm just off the Italian seaside town of Nettuno. The statue was brought ashore and placed in the local church where it remains to this day. It is celebrated locally as The English Lady or Our Lady of the Graces.

The Nettuno statue was found to be wearing 'two half shoes' made of England silver, as described by Thomas Thacker, steward in charge of conveying the statue to London in 1538, and on the back had words translated as Old English for 'Thou art gracious'.

The bronze image of the Ipswich Madonna on the wall in Lady Lane is by the Irish sculptor, Robert Mellamphy (who lives in the town), and was modelled in 1990 after a study of the Nettuno statue.

The modern Shrine of Our Lady of Grace of Ipswich is in the Anglo-Catholic church of St Mary at Elms (see below).

**Continue along Lady Lane towards the car park.**

The turning to the left is Chapman Lane, named for peddlers who frequented that part of the town in the 1700s. A chapman was a traveller selling magazines known as chap books, but later any peddler came to be called chapman.

Across the car park to the right is the New Wolsey Theatre on Civic Drive, one of the town's foremost theatrical venues. The Wolsey Theatre opened in September 1979 but went dark in 1998. It reopened in 2001 as the New Wolsey Theatre and has stayed successfully open ever since.

There is a café in the theatre and a good view of St Matthew's Church to the right and along Civic Drive from the front of the building. St Matthew's

*The Wolsey Theatre opened in 1979 to replace the Tower Street Theatre and relaunched in 2001 as the New Wolsey Theatre.*

became the church of the military after the cavalry barracks were built in St Matthew's parish in 1795.

Beneath the theatre frontage is an underground spiral car park which, when it was excavated, was the first of its kind to be built in England, using a new method of concrete construction. It is 56 metres in diameter and 14 meters deep.

The sculpture seen on the Civic Drive roundabout is *Ship* (1971) by Bernard Reynolds, which won the Sir Otto Beit Medal for Sculpture in 1972. It stood originally in front of the (now demolished) municipal buildings of the Civic Centre. (The site is currently boarded up, its fate undecided.)

The council offices moved to what is known as the Administrative District in Russell Road (Walk 6).

**Return to Black Horse Lane via the car park and then head south.**

Notice on the left-hand side the back entrance to the Museum Street Methodist Church (that fronts onto Museum Street).

Next is the 16th-century Black Horse Inn, which lends its name to Black Horse Lane, originally a house which opened onto fields and meadowland that led down to the river banks. There are said to be underground tunnels leading away from the Black Horse to St Mary at Elms Church and another to the Swan Inn on King Street (see below). One explanation is that they were

*Town guide with walkers on Black Horse Lane.*

*Early Tudor brickwork of St Mary at Elms' church tower.*

used by smugglers in the 18th century when the Suffolk coast was a hotbed of illicit trade whose perpetrators sought hiding places for their goods, thereby avoiding detection by the men of the Preventive service. With good access to the River Orwell, and a short hop across land to the River Deben, Ipswich was the centre of distribution. It was by no means unusual for smuggled goods to be stored in churches and parsons were not averse to enjoying the benefits of excise-free brandy, gin, tobacco or tea. The *Ipswich Journal* newspaper is full of accounts of those arrested for smuggling, many accused of frightening violence and even murder.

### At the bottom of Black Horse Lane turn left into Elm Street.

Immediately as you turn into Elm Street the impressive red-brick tower of the church of St Mary at Elms (invariably shortened to St Mary Elms) comes into view.

The bronze statue on the triangle of grass beside the church is *Tam* (1995) by Honoria Surie.

*Surviving piece of St Mary Elms churchyard adds to the ambience of Elm Street.*

*Fifteenth-century cottages, thought to be the oldest, longest-inhabited in the town.*

**From the top of the grass island are seen iron gates at the north-west of the church tower.**

Behind the gates lies the Cottage (three in one) that dates from 1467 and is the oldest occupied dwelling in Ipswich. The cottages are believed to have been part of the grand Tudor house that once stood on Westgate Street belonging to Thomas Seckford (1515–97), Master of the Court of Requests to Elizabeth I and Member of Parliament for the borough. The gardens extended southward as far as the churchyard, and the cottages survive from that period and may have housed those who looked after Seckford's stables.

**The entrance to the church is on Elm Street.**

There was an 11th-century church here dedicated to St Saviour, but in the early 14th century it was rebuilt and the new dedication adopted to celebrate St Mary. To distinguish it from the other Marian dedications in the town 'at the Elms' was added. The 11th-century doorway is the oldest structure still used for its original purpose in the town.

The tower was built around 1443 and has a diaper pattern that uses darker colour bricks in the design, a feature more usually associated with the early part of Henry VIII's reign. It must, therefore, have been somewhat ahead of its time architecturally. This raises doubts about the common belief that the bricks came from Wolsey's abandoned college dissolved in 1530 (Walk 7).

Thomas Wolsey was, however, born in the parish of St Mary Elms. His father Robert was churchwarden and Thomas was christened here.

A chapel at the base of the tower, which housed a statue of Our Lady of Walsingham, was badly damaged in 2010 when a fire broke out destroying its contents and the first floor of the tower. What long-term damage has been sustained to the tower has yet to be assessed.

St Mary Elms has a long-standing Anglo-Catholic tradition. In 1977 the Guild of Our Lady of Ipswich (later Meryemana) was founded. One of its aims was to re-establish a Shrine of Our Lady of Grace in the town. A replica of the Nettuno statue, carved by Robert Mellamphy (who also executed the bronze in Lady Lane), now stands in the church.

Memorials are found throughout the church but notice the wall monument to William Acton (died 1616), clothier, his wife and their children. William was a benefactor to the town library. The memorial was erected by his son John and depicts Death standing above the family holding a pointed dart.

There is a Sir Ninian Comper window in the north-east window of the aisle. It is dated 1904 and bears Sir Ninian's trademark strawberry at the bottom of the right-hand panel.

In the late 17th century Huguenot refugees from France were encouraged to come to Ipswich to establish weaving industries. In 1681 the Council turned to Thomas Firmin (1632–97), son of Henry Firmin, a baker of Ipswich, and his wife, Prudence. The family were parishioners of the Puritan preacher Samuel Ward (Walk 5) who accused Henry of 'erroneous tenets'.

Thomas Firmin was sent as an apprentice to a girdler and mercer in London but maintained close links with his home town. He set up in business in London and became a philanthropist, offering work to those affected by the 1665 Great Plague. At one time he employed as many as 1,700 spinners, besides flax-dressers and weavers. Influenced by his Puritan roots, he had highly developed sense of the religious and was, among other things, a founder member of the Society for the Reformation of Manners set up in 1691 to suppress profanity and immorality (manners then meant morality rather than etiquette).

On Thomas Firmin's advice, the first four families came from Norfolk and a ship was sent to Norwich to fetch their goods and chattels. The town's general council agreed that the Huguenots be lent £200 interest-free for one year. Charles II wrote to the bailiffs and burgesses of Ipswich to thank them for their charitable welcome to 'the poor French linen weavers'.

More Huguenots followed and in 1685 the Huguenot pastor Balthasar Gardemau was appointed Perpetual Curate at St Mary Elms. He was educated at the academy of Saumur and had a special ministry to the immigrants and also taught their children.

In 1693 the borough entered into an arrangement with fifty families of French Protestants who were skilled in the manufacture of lutestring (or lustring, a glossy silk fabric). They were encouraged to settle in the town by the Royal Lustring Company and were 'supported liberally'. But the enterprise ultimately proved unsuccessful. The town was in a state of depression and there was already a problem with the river silting up and the subsequent hindrance to shipping.

By 1702 there were few Huguenots left in Ipswich and when Defoe visited here in 1722 he found that there was 'no thriving manufacture'. Some of the immigrants were allowed to stay in the town where they made and sold hats and opened shops.

In 1709 some German weavers applied for permission to settle in the town but were told that 'by reason of decay in trade, and having no manufactory to employ poor people' they could not be accommodated.

St Mary Elms is one of those churches that aim to open most days and is renowned as one of the town's most welcoming.

On leaving the church, notice a plaque on the opposite side of the road recording Mrs Smith's Almshouses, which were erected in 1760 as a result of a bequest by a London widow, Ann Smith (sometimes Smythe), who left

*Mrs Smith's Almshouses plaque on Elm Street.*

£5,000 to be used for the benefit of 'twelve poor Women, of honest Life and Conversation, of the Age of fifty Years and upward, being Communicants of the Church of England as by Law Established'.

Refurbished in 2001, there are now eight one-bedroomed flats with access to a garden hidden behind the red-brick building. The incumbent and churchwardens of St Mary at Elms are the trustees and the original principles still apply.

**Continue along Elm Street, cross Museum Street before arriving at the junction with King Street.**

At the corner of Arcade Street to your left is where the Victorian author Jean Ingelow (1820–97) lived. Her father was manager of the Ipswich and Suffolk Banking Company (in Elm Street). Although a hugely popular best-selling writer in the 1850s, her poem *A High Tide on the Coast of Lincolnshire* is almost the only one of her many works now remembered. She was highly regarded by Tennyson and Ruskin, and there is a Jean Ingelow Society in America.

The archway was built on part of the Ingelows' garden and allowed easy access to the museum from the town in the 1850s.

Just along Arcade Street were, until recently, the offices of Birketts, the solicitors (now located a short way up on Museum Street). It was here that Wallis Simpson came after she had obtained her divorce on 17 October 1936 in a 17-minute court hearing at Ipswich County Hall. Mrs Simpson stayed at Beach House in Felixstowe for six weeks in 1936 while she waited for the divorce. The following year she married the by then former Edward VIII in France and became the Duchess of Windsor.

Immediately ahead is the yard of the 16th-century Golden Lion, which fronts onto the south-west corner of Cornhill. It was once the entrance to the stable yard and reached via St Mildred's Street (now called Lion Street) a narrow lane named for the ancient Church of St Mildred that stood on the site of the Town Hall.

The aforementioned Yarmouth coaches stopped here to change horses and the Golden Lion (known at one time as the White Lion) was then prized as one of town's principal hotels.

**Turn right into King Street.**

In King Street is the Swan Inn, a much older establishment than the inscribed date 1707, which refers to one of its many refurbishments. In 1664 a one-time proprietor, John Parker, gave £2 a year out of the Swan's profits to provide coal for the poor of the parish.

*Initials on the Swan Inn, King Street, opposite the Corn Exchange entertainment venue.*

On the left-hand side is the second Corn Exchange which was opened in 1882 by Mayor Frederick Fish. It replaced the first Corn Exchange which stood in the south-east corner of Cornhill. In the 1860s there were complaints that the old building was too crowded, especially on market days, and the Council purchased the King Street site. In 1888 the fruit and vegetable market moved there from Falcon Street where it remained until 1970. The last Corn Market (or Exchange) was held on 29 June 1972.

The building was remodelled and opened by the Duke of Gloucester in September 1975 as an events venue. The Grand Hall is used for touring shows, concerts, local groups, discos, etc. and the Robert Cross Hall for fairs and exhibitions.

At the end of King Street is Giles Circus, one of the most recent changes to the town centre, work having been completed in 2010.

*Detail from the much-cherished Giles statue in Giles Circus.*

*The Town Hall steps are a popular meeting place.*

The Giles' Family statue (also known as *Grandma*) has stood on this site since it was unveiled in September 1993 by comedian Warren Mitchell, a great friend of Giles, in the presence of Johnny Speight (writer of the television series *Until Death Do Us Part*) and the cartoonist himself, Carl Giles (1916–95). For many years Giles (as he was always known) worked in a studio overlooking the junction where he created his cartoons for the *Sunday* and *Daily Express*.

The statue was sculpted in fibreglass resin by Miles Robinson. It was funded by Express Newspapers who employed Giles for more than half a century, and for 17 years it stood within sight of Giles' first floor drawing office. Its new position is close to its original site but now sits atop a three-tiered plinth.

**Turn left onto Princess Street and return to Cornhill.**

# THE EASTERN APPROACH

Walk 2 is a circular walk that begins and finishes at Cornhill, taking in:
*Cornhill – Tavern Street – The Walk – Tower Street – St Mary le Tower Church – Oak Lane – Northgate Street – Pykenham's Gate – Town Library – Old Foundry Road – Carr Street – Upper Brook Street – Buttermarket – The Ancient House – St Lawrence Street – Dial Lane – St Lawrence Church – St Stephen's Lane – Queen Street – Giles Circus – Princes Street – Cornhill*

The walk explores the eastern streets and churches of the town. There are numerous cafés, restaurants and public houses along its route and, like Walk 1, nowhere is very far from the town centre.

**Leave Cornhill in an easterly direction along Tavern Street with Lloyds Avenue to the left and the Old Post Office to the right.**

*Tavern Street leads off Cornhill with Lloyds Avenue to the left.*

The bustling, commercial Tavern Street is lined today with a variety of shops rather than the numerous taverns that once littered this part of town. The shops, together with banks, offices and food outlets, dominate the pedestrianised street, continuing a long tradition of commerce and trade carried out by both townspeople and visitors, especially those conducting business through the port.

In the 14th century the meat (or beast) and poultry markets occupied an area between Cornhill and Tower Street. Like other parts of town, it would have been not only noisy, crowded and congested but smelly and dubious underfoot: in summer dusty and in winter wet, muddy and slippery with open sewers running down the middle of the narrow streets. Itinerant travellers and preachers, pilgrims, tradesmen, musicians and officers of the king all rubbed shoulders with tradesmen, taverners and friars from one or other of the religious houses.

Street theatre was popular and, besides musicians, there were mummer troupes, contortionists and acrobats mingling with street hawkers and the general melee of urban life.

On market and fair days the town's population swelled to more than twice the number of permanent residents, many arriving on foot from outlying rural areas or by sea.

Daniel Defoe visited Ipswich in 1722 and recorded that market days would see upwards of 600 country people on horseback and on foot arrive with 'baskets and other carriage', in addition to the butchers' and miscellaneous carts and wagons.

In the 13th and 14th centuries the populace was cosmopolitan, ever changing according to which ships were in port. Easily spotted were the prosperous wine merchants from Bordeaux, timber and iron importers, and merchants from Cologne and from French and Spanish ports. In mediaeval and Tudor times, colour played a large part in street traffic; although peasants wore mostly russet clothing, merchants and foreign dignitaries dressed richly in red, yellow and blue costumes designed to show off their social rank.

Tavern Street gained a reputation as a place where business was transacted and the proliferation of inns and taverns afforded an opportunity to meet the out-of-towners. Along with the cries of the vendors would have been heard the accents of the foreign merchants, and the sound of French-speakers would probably have been the most familiar.

By the late 16th century customers were able to frequent not only the taverns but the coffee houses and by the mid-18th century patrons could enjoy coffee, tea or wine together with the use of dining and card rooms. By the 18th century, though, the narrowness of the street began to diminish its effectiveness. When coach traffic began, the frankly unpleasant conditions into which the passengers were pitched on arrival caused operators to bypass the town altogether. It was enough that they endured the rigours of coach travel on pitted and potholed roads, in cramped conditions, with the added danger of highwaymen. Each Royal Mail coach had a guard on board for protection, armed with pistols and a cutlass. He also carried a horn sounded to herald its approach to an inn and to clear the road ahead.

Due to pressure from inn and shop keepers, a street-widening programme was begun in 1817 between Tower and Northgate streets and traffic returned once more. Previously its eastern end had been no more than 12ft wide.

In the early 1900s the era of the horse-drawn cab and street trams overlapped and the consequence was yet more chaos for Tavern Street. The Ipswich Transport Museum (see Useful Information and Contacts) has a creditable amount of historical information relating to the dawning and development of the mechanical age.

During the 18th and 19th centuries townspeople promenaded along Tavern Street, meeting friends and generally enjoying the ambience. On Saturday evenings there was street entertainment and, of course, the inns and taverns would cater for those whose thirst was encouraged by conviviality and sociability.

Taverns and inns always played a crucial role in the town's economy, and even in 1830 there were still over 90 taverns and public houses listed for Ipswich town.

As the town population expanded and public transport improved, the street grew ever more clogged with stalls, wagons, mail coaches and people.

So congested did it become in the 19th century that posts and rails were erected to keep out the wheeled carts and it was forbidden to ride horses through on market days.

*The Walk, halfway along Tavern Street.*

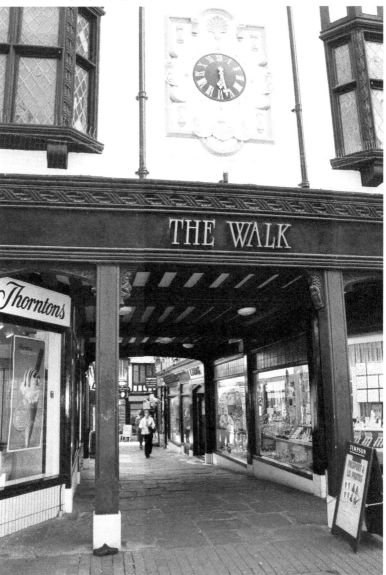

Because of its commercial importance in the town economy, Tavern Street was one of the first to be lighted: in 1793 Smythuril's patent lamps were installed, each one 50 yards diagonally distant.

**On the right-hand side (almost opposite the southern entrance to the Tower Ramparts Shopping Centre) is The Walk.**

The Walk, which leads to the lower section of the Thoroughfare, was designed by H. Munro Cautley and Herbert Barefoot between 1932 and 1933. In January 2005 it was granted special conservation status. The buildings are half-timbered reproductions and many of the narrow fronted shops have ornate carved details. Protected status is also extended to the Yorkstone paving.

In the late 19th and early 20th century there was a school of woodworkers in the town which specialised in producing imitation Tudor windows and façades, some of it so good that even experts were fooled into thinking them original.

After a distinguished military career in World War One, Major Herbert Barefoot, GC, ARIBA (1887–1958) joined the practice of Ipswich architect H. Munro Cautley in 1919. He lectured on building construction at the Ipswich School of Engineering (1924–28) and in 1928 became a partner in the firm Cautley and Barefoot. During World War Two he was a pioneer in bomb disposal and was awarded the George Cross in 1940 'for most conspicuous gallantry in carrying out hazardous work in a very brave manner'.

Henry Munro Cautley, FSA, ARIBA (1875–1959) was diocesan architect from 1914–47. In the 1930s he undertook a survey of the 500-plus churches in Suffolk and in 1937 published *Suffolk Churches and Their Treasures*.

A short way further along Tavern Street (to the left) is the entrance to the Ipswich Institute, established in 1824 as a 'Mechanics' Institute' by Dr George Birkbeck. It thrives today with a membership of around 2,500 who enjoy the benefits and facilities of the charity originally set up for the education of the inhabitants of Ipswich and surrounding areas.

**Turn left into Tower Street.**

In mediaeval times Tower Street was the Hen Market. It is hereabouts that a tavern stood that belonged to relatives of the 14th century poet, author and philosopher Geoffrey Chaucer (died 1400). A plaque can be seen on the wall beside the telephone boxes. Chaucer is known as the father of English

*Chaucer plaque on Tower Street, near the telephone box.*

literature and author of *The Canterbury Tales* wherein he wrote of fork-bearded merchants, sitting high on their horses, protecting the mouth of the Orwell.

On this corner, also, stood the famous Dods Coffee Shop, which occupied roughly the area of the former Chaucer family tavern. Among other things, Dods often appeared in advertisements carried by the Ipswich Journal as being the place to seek out various job opportunities.

Dods became popular during the 18th and early 19th centuries among race goers who took breakfast in the town before setting off to Ipswich Racecourse, between the Felixstowe and Nacton roads, returning later in the day to participate in cock-fighting matches in the Cock and Pye Inn on Upper Brook Street, which had its own cock pit with terraced seating for spectators. Taverns bearing the epithet 'Cock' invariably meant that cock fighting was one of the attractions offered.

The earliest mention of a racecourse was in 1710 when a Town Purse was offered for 'high mettled racers'. A covered stand was erected in 1727 with an inscription in gold lettering 'The Gentleman's Stand'.

Races took place in June and were attended by the local gentry and noblemen from beyond the county. During the Napoleonic wars they became a particular favourite with the officers of the 7th Hussars who were stationed at the Ipswich Horse Barracks.

A celebrated steeplechase, said to have been run in 1803 over four and a half miles from the Cavalry Barracks in Ipswich to Nacton Church, was depicted on four engravings by Henry Alken Snr (1784–1851). Known as *The Night Riders of Nacton*, it was subsequently alleged that the incident was entirely fictional and that Alken had illustrated an older event, albeit to good artistic effect and using Ipswich landmarks.

The racecourse became a housing estate in 1921.

On the left is the Old Rep public house, built as a Mechanics' Institute Lecture Hall in 1879. Many learned and respected men came here to pass on their knowledge and wisdom to town residents, one of whom was Charles Dickens, who gave readings of his famous works on his several visits to the town.

In the early 1900s the premises were opened as the town's first cinematograph theatre by John Poole. Poole's Picture Palace was highly popular but when the 'talkies' were introduced in the 1920s it could not compete with new purpose-built cinemas. During World War Two it served as a club for members of the armed forces. It opened as a Repertory Theatre in 1947 and renamed the Ipswich Arts Theatre. It closed in 1979 when the new Wolsey Theatre was opened (Walk 1).

The rudiments of the playhouse are still in situ and the Old Rep is a pleasant stop on the walk. The staff is friendly and if they are not busy will point out the salient parts of the old theatre layout.

Two doors up at Number 13 Tower Street is The Admiral's House, built originally in the 17th century, probably during the reign of Charles II, with the later addition of a Georgian façade.

Here lived Ipswich-born Admiral Benjamin Page (1765–1845) who retired to Ipswich after a distinguished naval career. His portrait, and paintings of six naval actions in which he took part, he donated to the town.

However, he was a man who liked a quiet life and did not take kindly to a street vendor, Thomas Hearne nick-named Must-Go, who sold watercress on Tower Street. In due course Must-Go was in receipt of a small pension from Admiral Page on the condition that he did not shout his wares near the Admiral's house.

In 1820 Admiral Page entertained the Duke of Wellington and in 1835 was made an Honorary Freeman of the Borough.

**Almost opposite stands the Civic Church of St Mary le Tower.**

The present church of St Mary le Tower is the fourth church to stand on the site, its Victorian character being formed in the 1850s. The first church, probably wooden, was endowed with 26 acres and flourished at the time of Edward the Confessor, as recorded in the *Domesday Book*. The Latin form of

*St Mary le Tower is open daily.*

its name *Sancta Maria ad Turrim* (St Mary at the Tower) indicates that it stood near a tower associated with the town walls that ran to the north. In 1200 King John granted the town its first Charter. The king's seal was set to the Town Charter on 25 May and on 29 June (now known as Charter Day) the townspeople gathered in the churchyard to hear the Charter read. They elected the first bailiffs and four coroners who all swore to keep their office faithfully 'and to treat both rich and poor lawfully'.

The following Sunday, 12 portmen were also elected to govern Ipswich as a free town and to maintain the prescribed liberties granted by the king (Walk 6). The townspeople were required to obey the officials in their duties of preserving their freedom against all but the king and assist them in their endeavours.

Walking through the churchyard towards the church entrance, it requires only small imagination to think of those who, on 12 October that same year, stood in assembly and saw for the first time the town seal, symbolic of the

*Entrance to St Mary le Tower, the town's Civic Church.*

*St Mary le Tower's 15th-century font: the lions are to frighten away evil.*

new borough and the freedoms it afforded. It meant that Ipswich could manage its own affairs without recourse to the king.

The church here in 1200 was the Romanesque building that had replaced the wooden Saxon building and is shown on the Borough Seal.

A guide to St Mary le Tower is available in the church, and a good look around is recommended.

Notice in particular the memorial to William Smart(e) (died 1599) on the north wall. William Smart was MP for Ipswich at the time of the Spanish Armada and added several endowments to the town's almshouses (Walk 5).

Its contemporary panorama of the town includes the spire that was blown down in the Great Storm that hit England on 18 February 1662. The spire was ripped off the church, turned upside down and its pointed end smashed through the church, shattering much of the interior.

At the west end are the Royal Arms of Charles II carved in oak and made in 1687 by Jonathan Reeve. In 1684 Reeve had been offered £6 for the job but it was decided, for whatever reason, that a set of £6 would not suffice. In 1687 the £6 offer was increased to £15 and Reeve was ordered 'to make them more graceful'.

It seems late for the alterations to have been commissioned as by 1687 the king had been dead for two years and James II was on the throne.

*Exit to Hatton Court and Oak Lane.*

**Leaving the churchyard, return to the Tower Churchyard and follow it round to the left, where it becomes Oak Lane which then leads to Northgate Street.**

As you leave the churchyard, notice the large white building opposite in Hatton Court which is currently Church's Bistro and Wine Bar. Hatton Court was named for the handsome and accomplished Sir Christopher Hatton (1540–91) who resided here. Sir Christopher was particularly distinguished for his dancing which attracted Elizabeth I's attention. He became one of the Queen's great favourites, so much so that he was accused of being her lover. He became her spokesman in the House of Commons and was one of the commissioners instrumental in condemning the Queen's cousin, Mary, Queen of Scots, to death.

On the corner of Oak Lane and Northgate Street stands Oak House. Although parts of the building date from the 15th century, the one on the site today was restored with elements from other Ipswich buildings and some newer work. It was originally a private house but between 1844 and 1855 became The Royal Oak Inn. The landlord of the Great White Horse (see below) hired all the rooms at the Royal Oak to accommodate the many 'bagmen' (travelling salesmen) whose custom he needed but whose boisterous behaviour offended his more regular customers.

Notice particularly the corner post showing a Tudor man and a blacksmith.

*Tudor man, detail from Oak House corner post on Northgate Street.*

*Pykenham's Gate on Northgate Street.*

**Walk a short way up Northgate Street.**

On the left-hand side is Pykenham's Gate built by William Pykenham, Archdeacon of Suffolk. A house for the Archdeacons of Suffolk had stood here on the site the 13th century but Pykenham wanted to make it grander and caused the gatehouse and wall to be built in about 1471. The brick gateway with a crow-stepped gable stands at the entrance to the Archdeacon's House and has a room above which would have been occupied by the gatekeeper. The Archdeacon represented the Bishop of Norwich, under whose jurisdiction Ipswich was until 1914.

The Archdeacon's House and the nearby Holy Trinity Priory were two places in the town which suffered the wrath of the mob during the Peasants' Revolt of 1381. On 16 June looted muniments were consigned to large bonfires at the priory, although the archdeacon himself was away at the time. There were show-piece public decapitations of rebels at Ipswich after the rioting was brought under control.

The gateway is leased by the Ipswich Building Preservation Trust from the Ipswich & Suffolk Club (established in 1885) who inhabit the Archdeacon's House.

The property behind the wall is private but on an organised town walk, or during the annual Heritage Open Day, it is possible to view the gatekeeper's house from inside the club car park. The timber-framed rooms above the gate were restored in 1982–83 by Ipswich Building Preservation Trust.

Opposite the gate is the Town Library, built in 1924. Ipswich was one of the first towns in England to adopt the 1852 Public Libraries Act and opened branch libraries to serve the growing suburbs.

On the corner of Northgate Street and Tower Ramparts is the Halberd Inn (now P.J. McGinty's) which stood immediately outside the old ramparts in

*Behind the bar inside P.J. McGinty's is a section of the old town wall.*

the vicinity of the North Gate and enjoyed brisk trade from those entering and leaving the town. A section of the ancient town wall can be seen behind the bar.

In the 1700s the Halberd had a steelyard (or stillyard) for weighing hay 'as just and true as any in England'. Hay was needed not only for the inn

*P.J. McGinty's, where the North Gate once stood.*

customers' own horses but also for the coaching stables a short way up the road in Neale Street (Walk 3).

In the 1830s and 40s there were over 65 independent carriers who ran private wagons to towns across Suffolk, Norfolk and beyond. Many of them left from the Halberd, including William Osborn who departed every Saturday at noon; Elijah Salter every Wednesday and Saturday noon for Aldeburgh; and John Sheppard every Monday, Wednesday and Friday for Colchester.

P.J. McGinty's has the reputation of being the most haunted pub in Ipswich. Its chief ghost is a monk from Holy Trinity Priory who was murdered and thrown down a well. Perhaps it was the very well that can still be seen today in the saloon bar.

The North Gate, also known as Old Bar Gate or, latterly, St Margaret's Gate, once straddled the top of the street to which it gave its name. It was the entry point for those coming into town from the north east. It was demolished in 1794 having survived 12 years longer than the West Gate.

Eastwards from here runs Old Foundry Road, named in honour of Robert Ransome's ironworks established in 1789. Robert Ransome (1753–1830) was a schoolmaster in Norfolk but after serving an apprenticeship as an ironmonger came to Ipswich to set up his own foundry. The Ransomes were a Quaker family and found kindred spirits in others in the town, such as the Alexanders and Gurneys (bankers).

Ransomes (later Ransomes, Sims & Jefferies) developed into one of the best known manufacturers of agricultural implements and gained a world-wide reputation for their famous Ransome lawnmowers. During the years of its existence the firm diversified into civil and railway engineering and the manufacture of electric vehicles (including the Trolleybus).

Another company was formed in 1869, Ransomes & Rapier, which concentrated on railway engineering, cranes and locomotive turntables. In 1904 the firm installed a revolving stage, invented by theatre manager Oswald Stoll, for the London Coliseum Theatre. It later built the revolving restaurant on London's BT Tower.

Among the many achievements of Ransomes & Rapier was their involvement with the first Chinese railway. In 1874 a steam locomotive was built for use in construction on the Shanghai and Woosung Railway and was the first to run in China. Two more locomotives were supplied and the railway was successful and even profitable. Sadly, quite soon afterwards the railway was sold to the local Mandarins who closed it and ripped up the track, ordering it all to be thrown into the river.

During 1914 the firm was involved in setting up the Australian railways and during World War One produced shells, guns and tank turrets.

More information about the national and international importance of Ransomes can be found at the Ipswich Transport Museum (see Useful Information and Contacts).

**Retrace your steps back down Northgate Street to the traffic lights at the junction with Upper Brook Street and Carr Street to the left.**

Now consisting mostly of shops, Carr Street has been reshaped many times over the years and served as the main highway to destinations eastward. In 1887 the Carr Street Improvement Company was formed to buy up old property for demolition so that the street could be widened.

It is the street's ancient history, however, that distinguishes it. Saxon pottery was discovered on the south side at the eastern end of the street and in due course became known as Ipswich Ware. From the mid-seventh until the mid-ninth century, *Gipeswic* became a significant exporter of Ipswich Ware, which was the earliest, and only, post-Roman wheel-thrown and kiln-fired pottery manufactured in Britain. The kilns were situated in and around the Carr Street area. Examples of Ipswich Ware have been found across East Anglia, Essex, Kent and Yorkshire as well as in settlements beside the rivers Nene and Welland (Northamptonshire). The full story of Ipswich Ware can be discovered in the museum (Walk 1).

**To the right is the eastern end of Tavern Street.**

At the tail end of the 18th century the town's original post office stood at the corner of Tavern Street and Upper Brook Street, creating ever more traffic and chaos. It faced the Great White Horse to which, from 1791, the daily mail coaches delivered and fetched the mail.

In 1824 a coach left Brook Street every morning at 8.45am for the Golden Cross, Charing Cross, London and one returned every afternoon (except Sundays), leaving the capital at around 1pm. The journey took eight and a half hours.

In the 19th century the town was alive with the comings and goings of coach traffic. The artist George Frost (1734–1821) spent his entire working life at the Blue Coach Office but his spare time was devoted to drawing his native Suffolk and recording the busy quaysides of Ipswich. He was a great admirer of Gainsborough (Walk 5) and knew Constable but his work tends to be overshadowed by both. Frost's work can be seen in Christchurch Mansion Museum (Walk 3).

Coaches held sway in Ipswich for much longer than in other places, due to the late arrival of the railways (Walk 6).

In the 1830s the postmistress was Hannah Goodchild, who opened the office to the public at 7am and did not close up until 8.30pm. Business was conducted through a hole in the wall. Day and night post would arrive and letters and parcels for despatch were sorted, ready for the next mail coach.

The London post arrived at 4am and was despatched every night at 10.30pm. Mail from Norwich and Yarmouth arrived every night at 10pm and despatched the following morning at 4.30am. Letters from Manchester, Liverpool and the north of England arrived every morning at 9am and despatched every afternoon at 4.30pm. Hannah Goodchild was, it would seem, a very busy lady indeed.

After the introduction of the Penny Post in 1840 the number of letters doubled necessitating the removal of the post office to larger premises in the thoroughfare and an increase in staff from Hannah Goodchild's two delivery boys.

**Turn briefly back onto Tavern Street and note the Great White Horse on the north side.**

The Great White Horse is the only surviving inn that can be traced in Corporation records to before 1571. Evidence exists for an inn or hostelry to have stood here since 1518 but undoubtedly its origins are much older. The White Horse Inn (the Great did not appear until the early 19th century) has

*Great White Horse on Tavern Street, still one of the town's iconic buildings.*

always been the largest and most prestigious in the town: George II stayed here in 1736 and Lord Nelson in 1800 (Walk 7).

When Tavern Street was widened in 1817–18, the old frontage of the inn was demolished and replaced by the white brick and stone facing seen today. Its chief claim to fame is an association with Charles Dickens (1812–70), for it was here that the famous novelist and commentator stayed on his several visits to the town in the 1830s. He came here first in 1835, the year of the Municipal Reform Act, to record the disreputable goings-on that then passed for electioneering and which later featured in *The Posthumous Papers of the Pickwick Club* (1836–37).

Dickens was very critical of the Great White Horse and in particular the stone statue of 'some rampacious (sic) animal with flowing mane and tail, distinctly resembling an insane cart-horse' which stood above the main entrance. He used the inn's idiosyncratic layout to good effect, declaring that it was famous in the neighbourhood 'in the same degree as a prize ox...or turnip...or unwieldy pig'. The rambling nature of the building, with its labyrinths of uncarpeted passages and mouldy, ill-lit rooms, resulted in the famous scene when Mr Pickwick's nocturnal wanderings led him mistakenly into a room where stood 'a middle-aged lady, in yellow curlpapers, busily engaged in brushing what ladies call their backhair'.

So uncomplimentary was Dickens about the Great White Horse that the landlord, William Brooks, threatened him with a libel action.

*Croydons 1930s frontage.*

*Art Nouveau panel on the old Croydons building.*

In 1902 the hotel was put up for auction and bought by a developer who intended to demolish it. Such was the outcry in the town that planning permission was refused and the Great White Horse survived.

Opposite is the old Croydons building, whose 1930s façade was modelled on that of the Ancient House (in the Buttermarket, see below). A painting of *Father Time* and other panels record the watchmakers and jewellers, Croydon & Sons, seen above the main entrance. The firm was founded by Charles Croydon in 1865 and continued as a family business until 1994.

Look carefully along the northern façade where you can spot a beautiful little square, Art Nouveau window. There is another on the Upper Brook Street frontage.

A little further along (on the corner of St Lawrence Street) is Number 44 Tavern Street; high on the wall is seen the Corporation Arms indicating the site of the town's water conduit from which local residents obtained their water. Arising from springs in the hills above the town, the water was carried through wooden pipes, examples of which can be seen in the museum (Walk 1).

**Return to Upper Brook Street and proceed south.**

A short way down Upper Brook Street on the left-hand side is the previously mentioned Cock and Pye building.

**Turn right into the Buttermarket.**

The Buttermarket is one of the most picturesque and famous highways in Ipswich. Markets have abounded along the Buttermarket over the years. At one time it was dairying (primarily cheese) from the west end as far as the Ancient House, after which it became the Fish Market (close to Dial Lane). It was not always so named. In fact, it only appears for the first time in 1621 and in the 1630s was still known as 'the fish market now used as the butter market'. Even after the butter market ceased to be held there in the early 1800s, the name stuck and eventually was applied to the whole length from Queen Street to Upper Brook Street.

It could as easily have been named Printer's Lane, or similar, as in the 19th century the Buttermarket became the centre for the town's printing industry, Ipswich being already renowned as the first town in the Eastern Counties to set up a printing press. In 1534 the publisher Reginald Oliver had a stall in the Fish Market, and a few years later Anthony Scoloker published the translated works of Luther and Zwingli.

In 1812 Stephen Piper set up as a bookseller, binder, stationer and letterpress printer, and others followed. By 1844 there were 18 stationers and booksellers operating in the town. Six of them were in the Buttermarket, including Cowells – established in 1818 by Abraham Kersey Cowell who purchased the established firm of Richard Nottingham Rose. The Ancient House was home to by far the longest surviving of the Buttermarket printers and booksellers, being occupied by a succession of proprietors.

Just along the Buttermarket on the right-hand side is St Lawrence Street, which is more a lane than a street. It takes its name from the church of St Lawrence (see below), but during the 14th century it was the cloth market and in 1343 was described as 'the highway called the Clothemarket'. A small reminder of the mediaeval clothiers is a pair of shears set in an array of flushwork on the church wall below the east window. It was a draper, John Baldwyn (died 1449), who provided the money for building the chancel.

Halfway along the Buttermarket is the Ancient House, among the best-loved of the town's ancient and historic buildings. There can be little doubt of the Royalist credentials of its one-time owner: the Royal Arms are the centrepiece in an extraordinary frontage of highly decorative pargetting.

Few buildings remain unaltered during their lifetime, but the Ancient House, or Sparrow's House as it was formerly known, is a prime example. It is believed to have been built in 1567, on the site of an early 15th-century structure, for George Copping, a draper and fish merchant. Its brick and timber structure extends down St Stephen's Lane, where there is a courtyard entrance (which can be seen from inside the building).

*The Royal Arms on the Ancient House along the Buttermarket.*

In the 1590s it became the property and residence of John Sparrowe and thereafter Robert Sparrowe, a bailiff (or portman) of Ipswich. The house stayed in the Sparrowe family for almost 300 years.

In the Civil War, the Sparrowes seem to have bucked the local trend of being 'for Parliament' and instead were Royalist, hence the grand Arms of Charles II above the main doorway. It is thought they were created in 1668, eight years after the Restoration and just before the king visited Ipswich. Two cherubic figures can be seen under the Arms (thought by some to be Adam and Eve), although no one knows for sure what they represent. On the great baronial or royal seals, however, there were often awkward background spaces which engravers were at liberty to fill with beasts or birds, but it is thought that nowhere else in the country do such figures occur in this context. As such, they appear to be an Ipswich peculiarity, perhaps the work of a 17th-century town art master.

The two cherubs turn up again at St Clement's church, where a Mr Bierly is credited with 'the kings armes' (Walk 7). The Royal Arms in St Margaret's church (Walk 3) show similar figures.

A story persists that Charles II lay concealed within the Ancient House while on the run after the Battle of Worcester (1651). No documentary evidence exists but the family had several portraits of the king and claimed a link of mysterious origins with the House of Stuart. Since Ipswich was a

Puritan stronghold, it is to be wondered if the king would take the risk of being found there, or perhaps one of the Sparrowe family thought it would be the last place his pursuers would look.

The rest of the pargetting is emblematic. Beneath the windows are representations of Europe, Asia, Africa and America (Australia had yet to be discovered). On the west side is a kneeling figure of Atlas with a long beard and supporting a globe on his shoulders.

The shepherding scene on the corner is a reminder of the great importance of wool to the town, so much so that Ipswich was made a Town of the Staple. Staple towns were set up by Edward III in 1353 and meant that only designated centres of commerce could handle wool, thus making the wool tax easier to collect. Staple warehouses held on to the goods until the tolls were paid. The town's Staple Seal is kept in the Borough Collection.

There is a possible nod in the direction of a classical interpretation, too, as the bucolic tableau might depict the shepherd Tityrus from Virgil's *Eclogue*.

The Ancient House had become a printing house in the 19th century and for over 100 years was a well-known bookshop. It is currently occupied by the kitchenware outlet Lakeland, with goods in 10 rooms on two floors.

Notice the face carved on the corner beam on the shop opposite Ancient House at the corner of Dial Lane. Corner beams (sometimes known as dragon beams) are usually upturned trees, the widest part of the trunk bearing the load of the upper storeys.

*Shepherd and sheep on the Ancient House.*

**Turn right into Dial Lane.**

In the 14th century Dial Lane was formerly known as Cook's Row. It was the custom that traders of particular callings should operate in one locality and here it was the cooks, or victuallers, the sellers of food who hawked their wares in this part of the old town.

The church of St Lawrence dominates Dial Lane but is the most enclosed of the town's church. The present structure was built in the 15th century and is noted for its flint flushwork, some of which has been recently restored. It is believed that the building was started with a donation by John Bottold (died 1431), who is buried somewhere in the church.

The 97ft-high tower is the most handsome in Ipswich. The first thing to notice is that the tower was originally open at the base. The north and south doors are now blocked off, but the original moulding can clearly be seen. It is worth stepping back to take a look at the highly decorative tower, much of which was restored in 1882.

St Lawrence was attended by the Sparrow(e) family who lived at the Ancient House and there is a wall monument to John Sparrow, a magistrate who died in 1762. The Sparrowes are nearly all buried in the family vault (in the churchyard) which has 'Sparrows Nest' (in Latin) on the tomb.

The church was declared redundant in the 1970s and is now under the care of Ipswich Historic Churches Trust. After a long search for a new use it is now a community centre and café and called St Lawrence Centre.

*St Lawrence church interior, which has a viewing chamber for the weekly bell ringing.*

*St Lawrence church tower, the town's most decorative.*

The five St Lawrence bells have been much in the news of late and are reckoned to be the oldest set of bells in the world, predating the five bells of St Bartholomew in London. They date from between 1450 and 1458 and have recently been dubbed Wolsey's Bells because Cardinal Wolsey would have heard them as a boy in Ipswich. Together they form what experts claim is the oldest medieval full circle set of their type in the world. The bells had been silent for two decades due to the poor condition of the tower, but in 2008 it was proposed to rehang them in a new steel and cast iron frame, 26ft (8m) lower than the existing wooden frame.

A public appeal was launched and the bells were taken to Whitechapel Bell Foundry in London to be cleaned and restored, where they were found to be uncracked and with their original clappers. The bells were hung so that they can be seen from the body of the church and on 10 September 2009 the sound of the medieval bells rang out for the first time in 25 years. At time of writing the bells are rung between 12.30pm and 1pm every Wednesday.

During the summer Pickwicks Coffee and Tea House provide tables and chairs in a paved and shady section of the churchyard.

**To reach the TIC go south on Dial Lane, cross the Buttermarket onto St Stephen's Lane and into Arras Square – the TIC is opposite the Buttermarket Shopping Centre.**

**To return to Cornhill, return to the Buttermarket and proceed westward to Giles Circus.**

Once in Giles Circus (Walk 1), look back down Buttermarket and notice the way the upper storeys jut out over the street. This was a way for mediaeval residents to extend their properties out into the street to discourage traders from erecting their stands too close. In those days, rubbish and worse was thrown from the upstairs windows into the street below.

**From Giles Circus turn right onto Princes Street and return to Cornhill.**

# WALK 3

## A WALK TO THE PARK

Walk 3 begins on Cornhill and ends at Christchurch Mansion and Park, taking in:

*Cornhill – Lloyds Avenue – Tower Ramparts – Crown Street – Neale Street – Fonnereau Road – St Margaret's Plain – Soane Street – St Margaret's Church – St Margaret's Green – Christchurch Mansion and Park – Henley Road – Ipswich School*

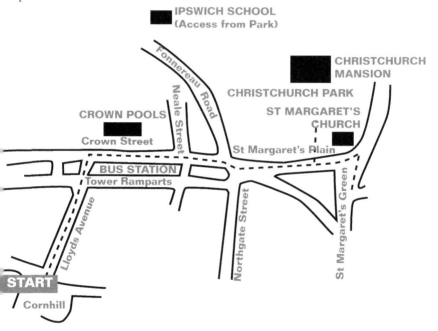

This walk stretches beyond the town centre, taking in the history of people and places as it goes. Once at Christchurch Mansion and Park there is plenty to discover in the museum, where there is a café and gift shop, and uncountable places to walk or rest in the park itself.

**Leave Cornhill on the north side, via Lloyds Avenue.**

*Lloyds Avenue goes north from Cornhill and was part of the 1930s plan to channel traffic away from Cornhill.*

Lloyds Avenue was cut through the existing buildings in 1929, widening the narrow Mumfords Passage sufficiently for vehicular access northwards from Cornhill to Tower Ramparts. The first vehicle passed through the arch in January 1930, but it is now closed to traffic other than a taxi rank.

Beneath the arch are two plaques: one commemorates restoration of the paving in 1982, and a second marks Ipswich as a Sri Chinmoy Peace Town on the occasion of the visit of the Oneness-Home Peace Run in 1999.

Notice the incline up to Tower Ramparts, which is a reminder that Ipswich does not lie flat but is surrounded by hills. The name Tower Ramparts commemorates the ancient defences that linked the main entrances (west and north gates) through which entry was gained to the town. In truth they were hardly defences at all since an assault on Ipswich was not likely to come overland but from the river, south of the town. Indeed, in AD991 the town was ravaged by Olaf and his Danish raiders and 'Danegeld' instituted across East Anglia, whereby landowners were required to pay protection money to the invaders. In 1010 they came again, this time led by Thorkell the Tall, and six years later the Danish King Canute sailed up the Orwell and Thorkell was appointed governor for all East Anglia.

There was possibly a tower or lookout of some kind in the vicinity as the nearby church is named St Mary le Tower (Walk 2).

*View of the market from Lloyds Avenue arch.*

The ramparts and accompanying ditches were constructed of earth in 1203, three years after King John's Charter (Walk 2), in all likelihood following the line of an older civic boundary. Murage (a mediaeval toll for building or repair of town walls) was granted to the town in 1299 and a licence given in 1352 to strengthen and crenellate the town with a stone wall, but nothing seems to come of it and the permissions were revoked. By the latter date the town authorities were likely preoccupied with the aftermath of the Black Death which struck the town in 1349.

Only a tiny hump of grass and a few stones, beside the ruins of the Blackfriars Priory at the junction of Fore Street and Lower Orwell Street, are what remains of the ramparts (Walk 5).

**At the top of Lloyds Avenue, Crown Street is straight ahead and Tower Ramparts bus depot to the right.**

The ancient town boundaries measure roughly four miles by five, and the distinctive mushroom shape of the Anglo-Saxon borough can still be traced in the street pattern of today.

Until the 1930s houses perched on the bank that once faced Tower Ramparts and backed onto what is now Crown Street. The houses were demolished and the ancient rampart, still discernible in the 1880s, levelled to create the open space that was originally a car park but is now the central

*Tower Ramparts bus depot (Electric House to the right).*

bus station. The ditch on the inside of the rampart was once known as Tower Ditches, then Tower Terrace and finally Tower Ramparts.

In the late 1970s, Tower Ramparts School, which opened in September 1899, was demolished to make way for Tower Ramparts Shopping Centre. The Shopping Centre opened in 1986, and its southern entrance is on Tavern Street (Walk 2).

On an island to the left is the Art Deco frontage of Electric House. Originally part of a corset factory, it became the Ipswich Electricity Supply Centre and was taken over by the Electricity Board in the 1930s.

A tunnel ran between Electric House and the old premises on Peel Street (at the top of Lloyds Avenue) but it was blocked up when the corset factory was demolished. It currently houses the Futon Shop on the ground floor and the whole building is currently earmarked for development.

The Mecca Bingo Hall opened in 1936 as the Odeon cinema.

**To reach Crown Street use the pedestrian crossing in front of Crown Pools.**

Crown Street is marked by Crown Pools, which has three separate pools including an eight-lane competition area. The street is supposed to have taken its name from a Crown Dairy that stood here in the 1830s. By coincidence, the street forms a 'crown' on the Anglo-Saxon street pattern, forming an arc shape above the ramparts. Many changes have taken place here over the centuries but Crown Street is an enduring reminder of the old town boundaries.

The Cricketers public house was purpose built by the brewers Tollemache in 1930 in the style of Helmingham Hall, which has been the home of the brewing Tollemache family since 1510. Look for the weather vane which has a batsman and wicket-keeper in play.

**Continuing eastwards the next turning to the left is Neale Street.**

In the 19th century this area was lined with stabling for stage and mail coach horses (Walk 2). Before the railways came in the 1840s the street would have been very busy, especially when the mail coach horses had to be harnessed and prepared for the turn-around of the London service. The 'post chaise' was the fastest vehicle on the roads of Regency England, although the galloping speeds took a heavy toll of the horses and their working lives were short.

The coaches had their own reputations to uphold, the 'Shannon' being described as 'coach par excellence'. It is said that the driver of the 'Shannon' was, at one time, John Cole who became the model for Tony Weller in Dickens' *Pickwick Papers* (Walk 2).

*The Cricketers on Crown Street.*

During the years that it took to extend the main railway lines from Colchester to Ipswich (opened in 1846), many businessmen took the 7am 'Quicksilver' coach from Westgate Street to Colchester in time to get the London train, returning the same day by the same route.

The upward slope of Fonnereau Road (next left) is immediately noticeable. Appropriately, the road is named for the de Fonnereau family, Huguenot refugees who descended from the Earls of Ivry in Normandy. They bought Christchurch Park and the surrounding area in 1735 and established themselves as one of the major players in Ipswich for the next 150 years (see below).

The Victorian housing expansion, brought on by the new wave of prosperity, began hereabouts from the 1850s onwards as evidenced by the architecture.

A short way up Fonnereau Road on the left is the Quaker Meeting House.

On the corner of Fonnereau Road and St Margaret's Plain facing Northgate Street is the Bethesda Baptist Church which dates from 1913 and seats 800. In 1999 the church acquired the adjacent premises on St Margaret's Plain that had for several hundred years been the Buck Inn (later the Running Buck) but which closed in 1984. Here The Key, a Christian-based centre of activity, was opened by former 'Manfred Mann' lead singer Paul Jones.

The Running Buck was one of five inns that stood outside the ramparts close to the North Gate. It was used by those attending the mediaeval Holy Rood Fair and by farmers and traders from the countryside.

**Continue along St Margaret's Plain (past the entrance to Christchurch Park, to which we will return) to Soane Street.**

At the end of Soane Street is St Margaret's Church. There was no church here at Domesday or when the Austin Canons established their priory where Christchurch Mansion now stands (see below). However, not long after the canons established the first priory chapel it was destroyed by fire and rebuilt some time before 1200 by John of Oxford, Bishop of Norwich. It was said to be relatively humble and resembled an ordinary dwelling house. By the beginning of the 14th century, though, the congregation had outgrown the chapel and the canons started to build St Margaret's in around 1307 in a corner of the priory grounds. By 1381 St Margaret's was the largest parish in the town.

One of the many glories of the church is the late 15th-century double hammerbeam roof.

Note the cherubs under the Royal Arms of Charles II (Walks 2 and 7). Another peculiarity of this church is a large painting of the Prince of Wales's feathers, dated 1660, although there was no such person at the time.

*St Margaret's Church off Soane Street.*

There is only one relic of the Holy Trinity Priory, a 13th-century coffin lid with raised cross. It is mounted on the aisle wall near the south door and is, perhaps, a memorial to one of the priors.

Among the church rarities is the text of a scroll on one of the 15th-century font panels which reads *Sal et saliva* (salt and saliva). It was a pre-Reformation baptismal practice to place salt in the child's mouth, and its nose and ears were anointed with saliva during the ceremony.

*St Margaret's 15th-century font bearing the scroll* Sal et Saliva.

In the churchyard are buried 440 victims of the Great Plague of 1665–66. A guide book is available in the church.

**Leaving the church note the Thingstead plaque on the triangular St Margaret's Green.**

The area around St Margaret's Green was once known as Thingstead, a Scandinavian word for a meeting place and one of the few reminders of the Danish presence in the town during the 10th century. It was here that the Holy Rood Fair was held, just outside the borough ramparts and close to the North Gate. The right to hold the fair, which took place on 25 September and the two days following, was granted originally in the 12th or 13th century to the Augustinian Priory of Holy Trinity (which stood on the site of Christchurch Mansion). At the dissolution of the priory the right to hold the fair passed to the Crown and eventually to the Withipoll family (see below). It is believed that the fair was last held around 1844.

Further down St Margaret's Green, just before the traffic lights on the left-hand side, is Manor House where Nathaniel Bacon (1593–1660) lived. Described as a 'pious, prudent learned man', he was the grandson of Sir Nicholas Bacon, lord chancellor in the reign of James I. Nathaniel was for many years the town recorder, also town clerk, and a key figure in Ipswich political life in the 17th century. His town records were published in 1884 as *The Annalls of Ipswiche, The Lawes Customes and Government of the Same*

*St Margaret's through the trees in Christchurch Park.*

collected out of the records books and writings of that town. He was a strong supporter of the Puritan cause but nevertheless regretted the execution of Charles I, recording in 1649 'the last day of January puts a sad period upon my pen'. Nathaniel Bacon was town recorder in 1645 when the Ipswich witchcraft trials were held on Cornhill (Walk 1).

**Head back towards St Margaret's Church, turn left into Soane Street and the entrance to Christchurch Mansion and Park is on the right-hand side.**

As you go, notice on the left-hand side Freemasons Hall, completed in 1870 and updated in 1911.

Opposite the entrance to the mansion note the timber-framed building on the left-hand corner previously known as the Old Pack Horse Inn. It was used as a guesthouse for visitors to the pre-Reformation Augustinian Priory of the Holy

*The Tau cross on Old Pack Horse Inn corner post.*

*The Old Pack Horse Inn once had its three gables side by side.*

Trinity. The corner post bears a shield that has a Tau Cross (commonly called St Anthony's Cross) carved on it with a sun and two moons for the Holy Trinity (which gives it the appearance of an anchor). At one time all the gables faced towards Crown Street but in 1936 its shape was altered to accommodate the change in road patterns and development of St Margaret's Plain.

*Soane Street entrance to Christchurch Park and Mansion.*

**Once inside the Park Christchurch Mansion is seen directly ahead.**

Christchurch Mansion was built on the site of the Augustinian Priory of the Holy Trinity that was established about 1160 by the Augustinian (Black) canons. It was dedicated to the Holy Trinity but also called Christchurch in honour of St Augustine's first English church, given to him in AD597 by Ethelbert, King of Kent. It was the second Augustinian house in the town, the first being St Peter and Paul on the Waterfront (Walk 7).

For 375 years, until it was suppressed by Henry VIII at the Reformation, the priory and its resident canons played an important role in the spiritual and material life of the townspeople and witnessed Ipswich's growth from a modest settlement to a thriving town. Like monks, the canons led a communal life but, unlike monks, they were priests whose purpose was to engage in public ministry of liturgy and sacraments for those who attended their churches. They ministered in the town churches of St Lawrence, St Margaret and others.

The habit of the Austin canons consisted of a black cassock, white surplice and hooded black cloak which caused them to be known as the Black Canons.

The priory owed its endowment to several men including Simon, son of Osbert, and Norman, son of Eadnoth (who gave the church of St Mary le Tower and lands both inside and without the ramparts). There were only seven canons to begin with, the number rising to over 20 in due course.

Holy Trinity Priory was suppressed in February 1537 after the royal commissioners had taken an inventory the previous summer. Nothing now remains of the priory complex, although a tower belonging to Trinity Chapel (on the site of the mansion) survived until the 17th century. In 1735 John Kirby published a book entitled *Suffolk Traveller*, wherein he writes of the tower 'the strong foundation of this steeple was within these few years undermined and blown up with gunpowder'.

At the Reformation, the priory estate was sold to Paul Withipoll, a London merchant. The Withipoll family had made good in the capital and also had considerable business interests in Italy. In 1548 his son, Edmund Withipoll (1512–82), began building the red brick edifice known today as Christchurch Mansion. It is said that Edmund Withipoll was glad to escape to Ipswich having slain his French serving man at his home in Walthamstow. His somewhat mercurial temperament led him into several disputes with the town bailiffs (particularly over 'rights of way' issues), although he was a man of letters with 'a measure of classical learning'.

Members of the Withipoll family were continually embroiled in disputes with the Corporation regarding rents, water, tithes, pew rents, fairs and

*The Norwich Early Dance Group re-enact a skittles game in front of Christchurch Mansion.*

various other matters. A 'Withipoll of Ipswich' was implicated in a public duel on 20 May 1598.

The mansion remained in the Withipoll family until 1645 when Sir William Withipoll died and it was inherited by his daughter, Elizabeth, and her husband Leicester Devereaux (later 6th Viscount Hereford). There was a certain discord in the family during the Civil War as Sir William stood for the King but Elizabeth had married an officer in the Parliamentary army. Devereaux was the great-grandson of Sir Robert Devereaux, 2nd Earl of Essex, Elizabeth I's favourite and High Steward of Ipswich, who was beheaded in 1600.

The pragmatic Devereaux was amongst those appointed to visit Charles II to invite him to return to England. In 1660 he was one of six peers accompanying the king home from exile in Holland. The king later honoured him by visiting Christchurch in 1668 when he played bowls on the ancient bowling green. The game is called bowls but is thought to have been more like skittles: a centre wood (or skittle) stands in the middle of a circle of eight smaller woods. The player throws the ball attempting to knock over the centre wood but leaving the outside circle upright.

Christchurch remained in the Devereaux family until 1735, when it was sold to Claude Fonnereau, a wealthy London merchant of Huguenot descent.

The Fonnereau family remained in occupation until 1894 when the contents of the mansion were sold and the estate put up for sale. The site was bought by a syndicate that aimed to demolish it. However, Felix Thornley

Cobbold (1841–1909), a banker whose business later became Lloyds Bank, bought the property from the syndicate and presented it as a gift to the town on condition that the borough purchase the remainder of the park.

Felix Cobbold was one of many in the Cobbold family who were at the forefront of Ipswich society, playing a leading role in the town's development and prosperity. Besides their brewing empire, the Cobbolds were instrumental in planning the Wet Dock (Walk 8) and put up their own money to bring the railway to Ipswich in the 1840s (Walk 6).

There is much to see in Christchurch Mansion, but the first is The Hall which was the main living room in early Tudor times as well as the dining area for guests. It runs the width of the original main part of the house and is two storeys high.

The mansion has rooms furnished in various styles from Tudor to Victorian periods. The Wingfield Room was built for the display of the panelling and over mantel taken from the town house of the Wingfield family formerly in Tacket Street (Walk 5). The panelling had been removed in 1870 to a private house but was acquired by the museum in 1929.

Among the varied collections is one of Lowestoft Porcelain manufactured in the Suffolk coastal town between 1757 and 1799. There are also displays of dolls houses, toys and games from the past.

The Wolsey Art Gallery has exhibitions throughout the year and the Suffolk Artists Gallery displays visual art from the Borough Collection. The mansion houses the most significant collection of Constable and Gainsborough paintings outside London.

Guide books and souvenirs are available in the gift shop and there are attendants on hand to help with information and directions. There is also a café that sells ice cream and other refreshments. It is also possible to order a picnic hamper from the tea shop next to the courtyard.

**Return to the Park.**

Christchurch Park extends over 80 acres and was formally opened to the public, free of charge, on 24 April 1895, the borough having acquired the mansion and park the previous year. The museum opened the following year. The park remains the town's most popular. It is Grade II listed in the English Heritage Register of Historic Parks and Gardens. There are 14 other Grade II listed structures within the park including lodges, gates, walls and an ice house (not currently visible but scheduled for a restoration project).

Until the end of the 19th century, sheep still grazed the grass although the small herd of deer that roamed the grounds, established by the Withipoll family, had by then disappeared.

*The Round Pond is thought to have once been a fishpond for the old priory.*

*Duck feeding food is available at the Round Pond.*

In addition to the open spaces there are croquet lawns, a bowling green, tennis courts and Lower and Upper Arboreta.

Once inside the park there are numerous walks and points of interest. The Round Pond can be seen to the north of the mansion and is said to be the remnant of one of the priory fish ponds.

A short way up on the right (the Round Pond to the left) is the Ipswich Martyrs' Memorial (Walk 1) which commemorates the nine Protestants who suffered martyrdom in Ipswich during the Marian persecutions.

*Goldfish in the Round Pond are a firm favourite with the children.*

*The mansion showing the proximity of St Margaret's Church, just visible on the right.*

Close by is the Reg Driver Visitor Centre. The centre was officially opened in 2008 and was named after James 'Reg' Driver, the first Chairman of the Friends of Christchurch Park, President of the Ipswich Branch of the Royal British Legion and an Ipswich Borough Councillor (1976–90). The centre maintains displays of information about the park, its history, restoration,

*The Reg Driver Centre (up the hill on right) has an Information Centre and regular town-related exhibitions.*

*Courtyard garden with 'Triple Mycomorph' (Fungus Form) by Bernard Reynolds.*

trees, plants and wildlife. It houses the park manager's office and has an education room for a series of seasonal exhibitions throughout the year. Any enquiries concerning the park should be directed to the staff at the centre.

In addition to the occasional exhibitions there is a permanent collection of items on show that were recovered in 2007 from the mud at the bottom of the Round Pond during a clean out. Among other things are several coins, a spoon, lead soldiers, metal buttons, a watch, bullet cases and a coronation coin of Edward VIII (1937). The latter has the caption 'Perhaps thrown away in disgust!'

Christchurch Park plays host to year-round entertainments and activities including popular music concerts, the Remembrance Day ceremony and events connected to Ip-Art (see Ipswich Borough Council website for details). The annual Ipswich Scout Group Charity Fireworks display is held in the park and there is to be a special

*The park is home to in excess of 100 different bird varieties, including ducks, geese and swan.*

*Springtime in the Park with the War Memorial in the distance.*

celebration on 5 July 2012 when the historic Olympic torch is brought to the town in the build-up to the London 2012 Games.

The Tree Trail leaflet has a map showing the whereabouts of over 20 of the more unusual trees in both the Lower and Upper Arboretum including a Cider Gum (*Eucalyptus gunnii*), which is the largest girth Cider Gum in East Anglia; Caucasian Wingnut (*Pterocarya fraxinifolia*); Cedar of Lebanon (*Cedrus libani*); and Coast Redwood (*Sequoia sempervirens*).

To the west of the Round Pond is the Suffolk Soldiers Memorial and further up is the War Memorial, which commemorates the fallen in two world wars.

**To visit the Upper Arboretum follow the path to the left of the Wilderness Pond with the Band Stand to the left and go through the tunnel.**

The oak beside the Band Stand was planted on the day of the wedding of HRH Edward, Prince of Wales, in 1866.

The tunnel is found beneath the extensive root system of a Holm Oak (or Holly Oak as it takes its name from an ancient name for holly) which is one of Britain's few naturalised evergreen oaks and one native to the Mediterranean region.

Along the walk notice the various plaques to past aldermen and mayors of the town.

*The Wilderness Pool was constructed in 1567 by Edmund Withipoll.*

*Tunnel to the Upper Arboretum in Christchurch Park which leads to the Henley Road entrance.*

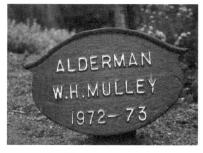

*Watch for the Alderman memorials throughout the park.*

There is another entrance/exit to the park on Henley Road, immediately opposite the entrance to Ipswich School.

Ipswich School was built in 1851–52, but its scholastic origins are much older having been established in the 14th century as a foundation of a merchants' guild for the education of its members' children. It was consolidated in 1482 when Richard Felaw, a local merchant and MP for the Borough, bequeathed his house to the school (in what is now Foundation Street). Known for many years as Felaw's House, it was demolished in 1963 as part of a slum clearance programme.

The porch and tower of the present school entrance are intended to reflect the style of the gateway to Wolsey's College in St Peter's Street (Walk 7).

On 4 July 1851 HRH Prince Albert laid the foundation stone for the building, having arrived in Ipswich the previous day by train. Unfortunately, as His Royal Highness left for the station in an open carriage, someone in the crowd shouted abuse at him, calling him a 'rotten old German'. On hearing

*Henley Road Park entrance, opposite Ipswich School.*

this Queen Victoria was definitely not amused and placed a 75-year interdict on Royal visits to the town.

One of the 16th century's more colourful headmasters, Richard Argentine (master from 1538 to 1558), instigated a revival of the curious mediaeval Boy Bishop custom. A boy was elected to perform the duties usually associated with a bishop during the three-week period from St Nicholas's Day (6 December) to Holy Innocents' Day (28 December). Argentine led the boy 'with his miniver hood about the streets, for apples and bellie-cheer'.

The Boy Bishops were given lead alloy tokens: four have been found in Ipswich and one can be found in Ipswich Museum (Walk 2).

Another master was Cave Beck (1623–c.1706), author of an early 'constructed' language on similar principles to Esperanto (1887). In his book *Universal Character* (1657), Beck proposed a universal language based on a numerical system 'the practice whereof may be attained in two hours space, observing the grammatical directions, which character is so contrived, that it may be spoken as well as written'.

Until the 16th century, Latin was the universal language and it is said that those exponents of universal characters, or language, got the idea from the Jesuits who went to China and used pictorial words rather than the letters of an alphabet.

On the frontispiece of the book is a portrait of Beck seated at a table in conversation, by means of his invention, with a Turk, a Hottentot and a Red Indian.

As chaplain to Viscount Hereford (of Christchurch Mansion), and tutor to the Devereaux children, Cave Beck was among the party which escorted the exiled Charles II back to England to his restored throne in 1660.

# IN THE FOOTSTEPS OF KING HENRY

Walk 4 begins on Cornhill and finishes at the Tourist Information Centre, taking in:

*Cornhill – Giles Circus – Princes Street – Coytes Gardens – Friars Street – Willis Building – Unitarian Meeting House – Cromwell Square – St Nicholas Church – Cutler Street – St Nicholas Street – St Peter's Street – Rose Lane – Curson Plain – Silent Street – Old Cattle Market – Dogs Head Street – St Stephen's Lane – TIC*

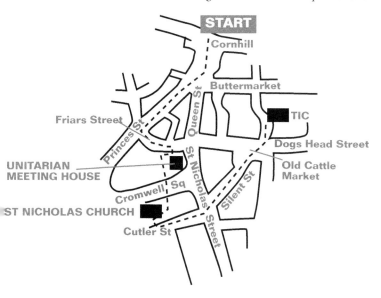

This walk explores the area south of Cornhill and discovers those places associated with Tudor Ipswich. Nowhere is far from an eatery and in the summer one or two restaurants spill out onto the pavements.

**Go south from Cornhill, with Giles Circus to the left, onto Princes Street.**

The architectural evidence of Victorian commerce is arrayed on either side of Princes Street, which reaches from the centre of town down to the railway station and the river Orwell. This was the first direct highway from Cornhill

*The Princes Street exit runs south from Cornhill to the railway station.*

to the lower part of town. Previously, in Anglo-Saxon and mediaeval times, north-to-south access relied on Brook Street (Walk 2), Lower Orwell Street and St Stephen's Lane (Walk 5).

The lower half of Princes Street was built in the 1840s (the bridge completed in 1849) but the upper portion took longer as it bore diagonally through a mesh of existing houses, gardens, orchards, streets and lanes. By the end of the century, Princes Street was synonymous with commercial offices, banks, insurance companies and building societies, reflecting the town's 19th-century prosperity.

**A short way down Princes Street, on the left-hand side, is Coytes Gardens just before No 31 Giles Place.**

Coytes Gardens is a remnant of the ancient jumble of streets and houses that once spread across this part of town. The small, L-shaped thoroughfare is built of setts (broken stones), similar to those surviving in the Old Sun Inn courtyard on St Stephen's Lane (Walk 5), but found nowhere else in the town. At the Friars Street end one can see central guttering laid down before the more usual roadside guttering.

In the 17th and 18th century, Ipswich had a reputation for fine gardens, vineyards and orchards, none more fine than those which once flourished here. Dr William Beeston started his 'physick garden' in 1721 and both garden and doctor became famous, attracting the attention of Daniel Defoe who described Dr Beeston as being 'exquisitely skilled in botanick knowledge'. The area around Coytes Gardens was laid out with spacious herb beds and shrubberies which, recorded the traveller John Kirby, made the town 'more airy and healthy, as well as more pleasant and delightful'. When Dr Beeston died it passed to his nephew, Dr William Coyte, whose daughter sold it for development.

During the second half of the 19th century Ipswich lost innumerable gardens and orchards to expanding urbanisation. Many of these can be seen clearly defined on earlier town maps. Almost all town houses had a reasonable plot of land running behind the road frontage. Grounds belonging to a Mr Sweet are mentioned as being on Friars Road in the 1890s and there was once a large garden attached to the nearby Unitarian Chapel.

Some of the hedges depicted might well have dated from mediaeval times, planted to denote property boundaries and help maintain privacy at a period when eavesdroppers would roam the streets listening under the unglazed windows, hoping for information that they could sell or trade. In 1416, four men were accused of being common night prowlers, and in 1422 one John Salter was named 'a common garrulator' whose evil words sowed discord

*Setts in Coytes Gardens (Friars Street end).*

among neighbours. In 1446 Richard Joye was before the Ipswich Sessions Court accused of roaming streets and yards all night 'secreting himself under the walls of inhabitants to listen to their secrets'.

Today Ipswich has over 2,100 allotment plots at 17 sites across the town including Castle Hill, where there is a resurgence of interest. The Ipswich Allotment Holders Association manages allotments for the Borough Council.

**After Coytes Gardens the next turning off Princes Street is left into Friars Street.**

Suddenly, three very separate strands of the town are evident: the name Friars Street is a reminder of a mediaeval priory; an imposing glass giant that is the Willis Building belongs unquestionably to the 20th century; and the Unitarian Chapel marks the religious divergence of the 17th century.

The Franciscan Friars, also known as the Greyfriars or Friars Minor, arrived in Ipswich in 1297, the house being founded by Sir Robert Tiptot of Nettlestead (c. 1228–98), sometimes Tiptoth, and his wife Una in the parish of St Nicholas. This was the last of the religious orders to establish in the town.

The 13th-century Franciscans carried an aura of internationalism about them as they had the reputation of being great travellers. They were itinerant preachers, ministering to the needs of those who employed them or from whom they begged. Both they and the Dominicans (Walk 5) were mendicants, meaning that they were forbidden to hold property and had to work or beg for their living. Their rule was poverty to the exclusion of all else, including learning. Poverty, decreed St Francis of Assisi, was an end in itself while education needed money, books and houses in which to keep the books. Some later sought release from the founder's strictures with regard to books and learning which caused strife within the Order.

The Greyfriars were popular among the people and as a result gained both money and gifts in kind. The people of the town brought their own service books and bibles and benefactors provided books for the choir in return for the prayers of the friars.

Both Sir Robert and his wife Una were buried in the Greyfriars' cemetery, the Pope having granted the privilege of burying friars and intimates there in 1250. Sir Robert was a Crusader and between 1270 and 1272, together with five other knights, went on the 9th Crusade with Lord Edward, later Edward I (1272–1307). Sir Robert would undoubtedly have been in attendance when Edward I visited Ipswich in 1277 and again in 1296 during the marriage celebrations of his daughter Elizabeth to the Count of Holland (Walk 1).

In 2010 investigative tests were carried out on bones from one of the burials discovered in the Greyfriars cemetery in the vicinity of Franciscan

Way and Wolsey Street. Unfortunately, much of the old complex was destroyed in the 1960s when Civic Drive and the Greyfriars Shopping Centre were constructed. However, some archaeological work was carried out in 1999, 2003 and 2006 when the cemetery was discovered and excavated.

The conclusions drawn in a recent BBC Two *History Cold Case* television programme caused great interest in the possibilities raised by assumptions made of one man's origins, namely that he was sub-Saharan. The radio-carbon date of the skull is very close to the foundation date of the friary and there are another possible eight skulls from the same origin. It has since been suggested that these were artisans from Italy who came to Ipswich with the friars or were men cared for in the Order's infirmary, perhaps off one of the many ships coming into the port from warmer climes. Ipswich was a busy port with trade and international crews from all over the world.

It is also possible that Sir Robert Tiptot brought back men of a sub-Saharan type who lived and died at Greyfriars. One of Sir Robert's fellow Crusaders, Thomas de Clare, is known to have brought back four Saracens to London.

The test skull indicated that the man had lived in Ipswich for around 10 or more years before he died of a spinal abscess and was probably disabled and infirm during the last few years of his life. He would have been well cared for at the friary since the Franciscans were known as apothecaries and grew medical herbs in the infirmary garden.

In another part of the cemetery one man was buried still wearing iron manacles. Discussions continue as to the origins of this and the other individual burials.

The friary was dissolved in 1537–38 and the site passed to Thomas Alvard, a cousin of Cardinal Wolsey.

**The Willis Building is evident to the right.**

The Willis Building was designed by Norman Foster Associates, built in 1973–75 and opened by Harold Macmillan. It was awarded a RIBA Trustee Medal for best post-war British building and in 1991 became one of the very few post–1949 buildings to receive Grade I listing.

The black glass walls reflect the surrounding buildings and contain over one thousand panels. Each pane of the toughened 'Antisun' bronze floatglass is approximately 3m x 2m and none of them open as the building is air conditioned throughout.

There was initial concern that the glass windows would be a magnet for hooliganism but the architect, Norman Foster (later Sir Norman now Lord

*The artistry of the Willis Building rooftop.*

Foster), organised a mock brick-throwing exercise during which the bricks bounced off the glass without breaking it.

Each of the three floors comprises around 1.5 acres (or 67,000 sq ft) with a rooftop garden, lawned to provide insulation. The lawn itself covers approximately half an acre.

*Dramatic escalators in the open-plan Willis Building.*

*The Willis Building contains almost 65,000ft of studded rubber flooring.*

*Princes Street and Friars Street from the Willis Building.*

The interior colour scheme of yellow and green is a constant source of wry amusement to Ipswich Town Football Club supporters since their team plays in blue and white, while rival Norwich City play in yellow and green.

The entire building is open plan – a new concept in the 1970s – and contains 140,000sq ft of carpet tiles.

**The entrance to the Unitarian Meeting House is off Friars Street.**

The Unitarian Meeting House was built in 1699–1700 as the Presbyterian Meeting House. In 1662, an Act of Uniformity required that Church of England religious services be conducted in accordance with the revised *Book of Common Prayer*. Those clergy who refused to conform were removed from their livings and gained the name 'nonconformist'. Legislation over the following years worked in favour of the Established Church and against nonconformity. A law was passed in 1664 that outlawed meetings of more than five persons who were not members of the same household and the following year the Five Mile Act banned nonconformist ministers from coming to within five miles of any city, town or parish where they had previously preached.

There is a peep hole on the inside of the east door used by the early Presbyterian Dissenters to make sure that it was safe to leave the Meeting

*The Meeting House reflected in the Willis Building.*

*The hipped roof of the Unitarian Meeting House from the top of the Willis Building.*

House without being observed. It looks across a courtyard and through a gap onto St Nicholas Street. The house was built after the 1689 Toleration Act, when the Ipswich congregation was founded, which gave nonconformists the

*One of the Meeting House's several elliptical lunettes.*

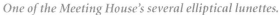

*View through the Meeting House spy hole across the courtyard to St Nicholas Street.*

right to have their own places of worship and engage their own preachers. But old habits die hard and it still paid to be aware of those who watched to see who in the town attended the Meeting House.

The courtyard pre-dates the Meeting House and is characteristic of a one-time Ipswich townscape.

The building has a hipped roof – a technique which avoids a very high single roof.

Once inside, notice the original box pews, the pulpit carved in the style of Grinling Gibbons, a Dutch 17th-century candelabra and a clock from an even earlier date.

Wig pegs can be seen in some of the pews: men were allowed to remove their wigs if it was very hot and the sermons were long. Families often rented their pews and the 'pew rents' were a source of church income. Sometimes locks were fitted on the inside of the pew door so that only those who paid the rent got the pew!

The pillars are thought to have been ships' masts.

The Meeting House is usually open to the public on Tuesday, Thursday and Saturday between May and September and during the annual Heritage Open Days. Precise information can be found on its website or from the TIC.

**Return to Friars Street and turn left along the path beside the Willis Building (on the right) towards Cromwell Square.**

*The Millennium Obelisk, which stands between the Meeting House and the Willis Building.*

On the left is the Millennium Obelisk. Its four sides represent: the Millennium, the 300th anniversary of the Unitarian Meeting House, the 25th anniversary of the Willis Building and the 800th anniversary of the Ipswich Charter (Walk 2).

**Once beyond the shadow of the Willis Building, Cromwell Square car park is straight ahead.**

The square was once Cromwell Street and takes its name from Thomas Cromwell (*c.*1485–1540), who in 1524 entered the service of Thomas Wolsey. Cromwell was a strong advocate of the English Reformation and became known as the 'Hammer of Monasteries'. He assisted Wolsey in the dissolution of some 30 monasteries to raise funds for Wolsey's Ipswich and Oxford Colleges (Walk 7), and he later became King Henry VIII's chief advisor in succession to Wolsey.

Cromwell was one of those sent to Ipswich by Wolsey in 1528 to organise the pageant to the Shrine Chapel as part of the opening ceremony of the ill-fated Cardinal College (Walk 7). Inevitably, like Wolsey before him, he fell foul of the king and was condemned without trial and executed on 28 July 1540.

In the north-east corner of the square is a memorial erected to England rugby legend Prince Alexander Obolensky (1916–40), known as the 'Flying Prince' because of his pace along the wing. He scored a famous try in England's first-ever defeat of the New Zealand All Blacks at Twickenham in 1936. Prince Obolensky and his family escaped from Russia during the 1917 Revolution, his father having been commander of the Tsar's Imperial Horse Guards in St Petersburg. Obolensky later joined the RAF and died during World War Two when his Hurricane fighter plane crashed. He is buried in Ipswich close to where he died. He was aged 24.

The Flying Prince *in the corner of Cromwell Square.*

*Access path to Cromwell Square and the St Nicholas Centre and Sanctuary Restaurant.*

The unveiling of the statue in 2009 was witnessed by Prince Alexander's niece, Princess Alexandra Obolensky, accompanied by Prince Andrey and Princess Felizitas.

On the far side of the Cromwell Square car park is another of the town's mediaeval churches, St Nicholas', with the modern St Nicholas Centre and Sanctuary Restaurant incorporated into its surrounds by means of a glass hub. The Anglican Diocese of St Edmundsbury and Ipswich have had their offices here since the late 1900s.

St Nicholas' Church was built in the early 14th century on the site of a Saxon church dedicated to St Michael (which is mentioned in *Domesday Book*). It was here that Thomas Wolsey's mother and father were buried and his father left a bequest for the upkeep of the church.

The interior of the church is well worth a visit. If the Sanctuary Restaurant is open, ask to be shown the access door. Notice particularly the chancel which contains fragments of carved stonework, some of which are almost certainly Saxon, making them the oldest example in Ipswich. Here can be seen St Michael fighting the dragon, a semi-circular representation of a boar, and a group of stones thought to portray the apostles (all likely to have survived from the old church).

St Nicholas' church is in the care of the Ipswich Historic Churches Trust. From the footpath round the church, walk through the churchyard onto Cutler Street, turning left.

*View down to St Nicholas Church.*

**At the junction of Cutler Street, St Nicholas Street is to the left and St Peter's Street to the right (now known as Curson Plain).**

Notice down St Nicholas Street the mix of authentic and fake Tudor buildings. Usually, if the timbers are straight they date from the 1930s

*St Michael and the Dragon in St Nicholas' Church.*

onwards but even that is uncertain as some of the wood that was rescued from buildings demolished in the 1920s and 30s was used in new construction. Numbers 10 to 12 (currently Orissa) have a little bit of old Ipswich timber. Ipswich has a jumble of architectural styles but foxes the visitor further with a number of ancient buildings moved from their original sites to another part of town. Some, for example the Merchant House (see below) were reassembled with an eye to their original form, though more often they were constructed using a mix of old and new.

There are also several older jettied buildings on St Nicholas (Mimosa is a good example) from which the householder threw his rubbish out onto the street.

Look for The Ipswich Society Blue Plaque at 41 St Nicholas Street to VS Pritchett (1900–97). Sir Victor Sawdon Pritchett CH CBE (1900–97) was an Ipswich-born writer and critic particularly known for his short stories. His most famous non-fiction work is *A Cab at the Door* (1968), his autobiography, where he writes 'I was born in lodgings over a toy shop in the middle of Ipswich'. His father opened a stationer's shop in Rushmere which unfortunately did not meet with success and the family moved to Yorkshire, the first of many such moves that necessitated a cab waiting at the door. By the time Victor was 12 the family had moved 14 times. They returned to Ipswich several times, for varying lengths of stay, during Victor's early life.

A short way down St Peter's Street on the left is Rose Lane. It was named for the 17th-century Rose Inn that once stood here but, more importantly, it once formed the northern boundary of lands belonging to the Priory of St Peter and St Paul (Walk 7). It was previously known as Curson Lane, being one of the lanes bordering Lord Curson's mansion (see below).

Opposite the Rose Lane entrance is The Sailor's Rest, a unique (to Ipswich) William and Mary house built circa 1700. From 1925 to 1957 it was used by the British and Foreign Sailors' Society.

Looking down St Peter's Street there are timber-framed buildings on the east side. Timber and brick were used throughout the town because there was little local stone available. Those on the west side were demolished in a road-widening scheme to facilitate the trolley buses.

Halfway down on the left-hand side is a Tudor courtyard (now a restaurant) and just one of scores that at one time led off the main street. Notice the door opening up the wall through which goods could be unloaded straight into the loft.

**Cross to Curson Plain [in front of Wolsey statue].**

The number of courtiers and members of the household from Ipswich in the royal circle would now earn the epithet 'Ipswich mafia' and, one way or another, the town would be well known to the king. His sister Mary and her husband Sir Charles Brandon were resident for a while; it was the birthplace of his Chancellor, Cardinal Wolsey; Sir Humphry Wingfield and his nephew Sir Anthony Wingfield both had houses here (Walk 5), as did Lord Curson, with whom both he and Queen Katherine stayed. Sir William Sabyn lived here (Walk 7) and Dr Edmund Harman (1509–77), his protégé, was born in the town.

Dr Harman was barber-surgeon to Henry VIII and a substantial beneficiary in Henry's will. He was born in Ipswich 'of merchant stock', the second son of Robert Harman also of Ipswich. Dr Harman is depicted in the famous painting by Holbein the Younger showing Henry VIII with a group of eminent medics. In 1540 the king approved the union of the Barbers (of which Dr Harman was a leading member) and the Surgeons to form the Company of Barber-Surgeons. There are two paintings of Henry and his medical team, in one Dr Harman is bearded and in the other clean shaven. Curiously, X-rays have shown that both portraits were once bearded but one had been tampered with: was someone shaving the king's barber?

Lord Robert Curson (1460–1534/35) built a residence off Silent Street in about 1500 with a spacious garden and a 'strong and stately brick porch', or portico, which protruded into the street. Lord Curson served under Sir Charles Brandon during the French wars and was one of those who accompanied Henry VIII to the Field of the Cloth of Gold in 1520 (as did Sir Anthony Wingfield, Walk 5). Lord Curson knew Wolsey only too well since the Cardinal had made it known that he wished to make Curson's home his own when his proposed college was up and running. Curson, though, played a waiting game by asking for three years grace before handing over his mansion. Before the three years were up, however, Wolsey had fallen and his Ipswich college died with him (Walk 7).

Curson was an adventurer and something of a chancer and had a very colourful career, once escaping with his head after being sent to the Tower of London accused of treachery against the king. When he died, Lord Curson was buried in 'a magnificent tomb' at Greyfriars Priory. At the Dissolution the tomb was removed to St Peter's but is now lost.

All that is left of Lord Curson's mansion complex is Curson Lodge, on the corner of Silent Street and St Nicholas Street, and the adjoining bookshop. The two were built as one building around 1500 (at the same time as the mansion), although it is possible the lodge end had been a merchant's house and shop which was incorporated into the new building. It stood opposite the grand house to serve as a high class guest or lodging house in which to accommodate Curson's visitors. The ground floor hall and a suite of lodging chambers on the first floor were accessed by a gallery at the rear.

**CURSON LODGE**

THIS EARLY-TUDOR BUILDING IS A RARE SURVIVAL OF A MEDIAEVAL INN.

THE SURVIVING RANGE ALONG SILENT STREET WAS ALWAYS INTENDED
FOR THIS PURPOSE. THE CORNER PROPERTY OF ST NICHOLAS STREET
MAY HAVE BEEN USED AS A MERCHANT'S HOUSE AND SHOP. THIS WAS
LATER ABSORBED BY THE INN. AN IMPRESSIVE GROUND-FLOOR HALL AND
A SUITE OF LODGING CHAMBERS ON THE FIRST FLOOR WERE ACCESSED
FROM A GALLERY AT THE BACK.

THE BUILDING WAS RESTORED IN 2007 BY
THE IPSWICH BUILDING PRESERVATION TRUST

NEAR THIS 15TH. CENTURY HOUSE
ON THE OPPOSITE SIDE OF THE WAY
STOOD IN 1472 THE HOME OF
ROBERT AND JOAN WOLSEY,
WHERE THE GREAT CHILD OF HONOUR
**THOMAS WOLSEY.**
CARDINAL. ARCHBISHOP. CHANCELLOR,
PASSED HIS BOYHOOD.
IN HIS POWER AND PRIDE
HE RANKED HIMSELF WITH PRINCES
AND TROD THE WAYS OF GLORY.
IN HIS FALL
HE DIED A HUMBLE MAN
AT LEICESTER ABBEY
ABOUT THE HOUR OF EIGHT
ON THE MORNING OF NOVEMBER 29TH 1530
AND WAS THERE BURIED AT DEAD OF NIGHT

*Plaque on St Nicholas Street marking the childhood home of Thomas Wolsey.*

On the door of Curson Lodge, facing St Nicholas Street, is a plaque proclaiming the whereabouts of Thomas Wolsey's boyhood home, in a house on the opposite site of the road.

Thomas Wolsey (c.1471–1530) is considered to be the most famous 'son of Ipswich'. His statue in Curson Plain is the town's tribute to a man whose ambition took him to London where he became cardinal-minister to Henry VIII. He came to dominate the political and ecclesiastical life of Tudor England from 1515 to 1529 yet he was always dogged by his humble origins.

He was born the son of an Ipswich butcher, grazier and merchant who married into the Daundy family. Joan Daundy's brother Edmund was bailiff, Member of Parliament and merchant and is credited with paying for his nephew's education firstly at Ipswich and then at Magdalen College, Oxford.

Wolsey was ordained priest in 1498 and went on to become chaplain, first to the Archbishop of Canterbury and then to the Governor of Calais, where he met Henry VII. The king distrusted the nobility and appointed Wolsey Royal Chaplain. Thus, when Henry VII died in 1509 and Henry VIII acceded to the throne, Wolsey was already a familiar face at court. He was appointed to the post of Almoner, which gave him a seat on the Council, and gradually earned the trust of the new young king. But in spite of his elevated status he was never accepted by the aristocracy within the royal circle. His influence was considerable and far reaching, but stemmed only from the fact that he had the king's ear.

His eventual fall from power stemmed from his inability to satisfy the king's demands and in particular the monarch's desire to annul his marriage to Katherine of Aragon and thereafter to marry Anne Boleyn. Unable to bring this about, Wolsey quickly lost the king's protection: his possessions were passed to the crown and charges of treason brought against him. He was arrested in York and taken under guard to London, but while at Leicester he died suddenly in November 1530.

Unfortunately, in spite of pleas to the king, the Cardinal College of St Mary that he had founded in the town during 1527–28 did not survive his downfall. He begged Henry 'humbly, on my knees with weeping eyes' to take care of his two colleges at Oxford and Ipswich but only the Oxford one survived (Walk 7).

In Shakespeare's *King Henry VIII*, the Gentleman Usher Griffith and Queen Katherine discuss Wolsey's death, the former observing:

'Those twins of learning that he rais'd in you,
Ipswich and Oxford!  One of which fell with him,
Unwilling to outlive the good that did it;
The other, though unfinish'd, yet so famous.'

*Cardinal Wolsey statue, unveiled on 29 June 2011.*

The Wolsey Statue is by sculptor David Annand and was unveiled on Charter Day, 29 June 2011.

*Curson Plain is the new appellation for the site of the Wolsey statue.*

## Leave Curson Plain and go along Silent Street.

The unusually named Silent Street is another Ipswich conundrum. No one knows for sure why it is so called but it was established by at least 1764 and possibly sooner. The name has stuck in spite of efforts to rename it when in the 19th century Silent Street led to the Provision Market. For a time it became known as New Market Street but reverted when the market was demolished in 1897.

The most popular explanation is that when the surface was cobblestones it was covered with straw so as to muffle the sound of rattling carriage wheels and horses' hooves. Thus it became a comparatively silent street. During the Dutch wars, Lord Curson's house became a hospital for the sick and wounded and perhaps they craved relief from the constant noise of traffic.

Another theory is that the street suffered badly during the Great Plague which reached Ipswich around 1665–66 and thereafter became 'silent'. At least 35 seamen died in the King's Hospital at Curson House.

There is always the possibility that when Lord Curson built his mansion he required the street be, if not silent, then at least quiet. There is no way of knowing what it was called when Henry VIII's queen, Katherine of Aragon (1485–1536), came here on pilgrimage in 1517, or when the king himself visited Lord Curson and paid homage at the Shrine Chapel of Our Lady of Grace (Walk 1).

When Queen Katherine visited the Shrine Chapel she went there immediately on arrival, escorted by the Town Bailiffs. She stayed firstly with Sir Anthony Wingfield at Brooks Hall and then 'honoured Lord Curson with her company' the following day. The day she left, the Queen rose at six o'clock and went again to the chapel. She rode on horseback both going to and departing from the chapel and was escorted to the town boundaries by officers of the Corporation.

Henry VIII came to stay with Lord Curson in 1522 and, at dawn, went to the Chapel of Our Lady of Grace where he 'made oblations' and heard Mass. Might the king have strolled along Silent Street, enjoying the peace and quiet?

Moving along Silent Street the Merchant House, with a glazed courtyard, is on the left-hand side. It was moved to this spot from Star Lane when the Star Lane Gyratory road system was created in the 1980s. It was dismantled and the timbers labelled appropriately. However, it was stored in a barn for some years before being reassembled on Silent Street. When it was originally moved, whoever put the carpenter's numbering on the wood used an impermanent marker so that when they came to reassemble it all the figures had disappeared, while the labels had been eaten by mice. Happily, there were enough skilled people who could piece it together.

The original windows can be seen along the west wall: they were pre-glass and would have had shutters. On the far side the old timbers can be viewed through the glass panel.

**Continue along Silent Street which opens onto the Old Cattle Market – to reach the TIC cross Falcon Street with Dogs Head Street on the right.**

On the corner near the pedestrian crossing is the Plough Inn, another of the town's long-established drinking houses. The Plough lost a third of its frontage when Dogs Head Lane (now Street) was widened in the 1880s.

Ipswich is proud of its unusually named Dogs Head Street that derives its name from the Dog's Head in the Pot Inn that once stood at the junction with Upper Brook

*The Ipswich Dog's Head sign is likely to have been similar to this rare survivor of a Dog's Head (Cuming Museum, The London Borough of Southwark).*

*The Plough beside the bus depot with The Mill in the background.*

Street and Tacket Street. Its original name was likely to have been Dog's Head in the Pottage Pot and, as such, a rare survivor outside London where it had been a popular inn name since the 15th century. The name reproached those slovenly housewives who, rather than wash their pots under the pump, put them down for the dog to lick.

The name would have been familiar to Charles Dickens who no doubt saw it on one of his several visits. He knew of another Dogs Head in Blackfriars Road (London) and wrote of 'the likeness of a golden dog licking a golden pot over a shop door'. In Victorian times the sign was used by ironmongers who made 'dogs' for the fire and pots to hang over it.

There is also a long-established tradition that the Ipswich inn was named in honour of the Dutch contingent who came to town for the wedding of Princess Elizabeth in 1297 (Walk 1). The precise reason is not entirely clear but there is said to be a Dutch tradition that anyone late for dinner is said to 'find the dog in the pot', thus encouraging punctuality.

The TIC is along St Stephen's Lane in St Stephen's Church on the right opposite the Buttermarket Shopping Centre.

Park & Ride and town bus stops are found in front of Pal's Bar and county buses go from the Turret Lane depot opposite Pal's Bar.

# WALK 5

## FRIARS AND DISSENTERS

Walk 5 is a circular walk that starts and finishes at the Tourist Information Centre, taking in:

*TIC – St Stephen's Lane – Arras Square – Old Cattle Market – Falcon Street – Dogs Head Street – Lower Brook Street – Foundation Street – Tooleys Court – Blackfriars Ruins – Wingfield Street – Orwell Place – Tacket Street – Cox Lane – St Pancras Church – Christ Church – Dogs Head Street – TIC*

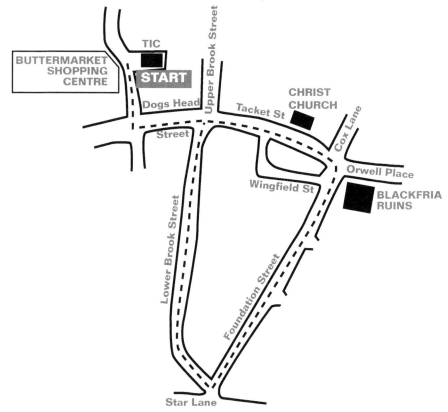

This walk explores the origins of Ipswich, introduces some of the town benefactors and discovers a little of the history of the mediaeval Carmelite and Dominican religious orders and a Meeting House of the dissenting nonconformists of the 17th century. Like previous walks, the town centre is never very far away and there are plenty of cafés along the way.

Standing outside the Tourist Information Centre at the top of St Stephen's Lane and off Arras Square is a good place to discover Ipswich's historical roots, as it was here that the earliest version of East Anglia's first economic capital took shape. Archaeology has proved that since at least early Anglo-Saxon times people have been working and living in and around St Stephen's Lane. The intriguing archaeological story can be studied more fully in the Ipswich Story permanent exhibition at Ipswich Museum (see Walk 1) on High Street.

St Stephen's Lane was then an important highway linking the river with the town's marketplaces and was a northward route out of town (although this was later curtailed when the town ramparts were built). It also led to, and from, the gates of the Augustinian Priory of Peter and Paul (Walk 7). All traces of the wooden houses that once lined it are gone, although the foundations for buildings, probably shops, have been found, as well as evidence of orchards.

From AD560–580, Ipswich was a wealthy community by the standards of the time and became a trading place of renown, with the port and associated trades connected to the wider rural network inland. It is clear that the port traded with the Rhineland, Flanders and Northern France and by the seventh century was one of the major Anglo-Saxon emporia. Towards the end of the

*Shaded seating in Arras Square.*

seventh century the settlement known as *Gipeswic* that had been laid down on the south bank of the River Orwell began expanding northwards. Evidence for the town's growth depends greatly on archaeological excavations carried out on the Anglo-Saxon burial site beneath the Buttermarket Shopping Centre in the 1980s and a second site at Boss Hall (now a business park to the north-west of the town).

The Anglo-Saxon cemetery that lies beneath the Buttermarket Shopping Centre was in use between the 6th and 8th century and provided evidence of the old custom of burial with possession. It yielded copper alloy artefacts, silver and glass beads, pendants and amber, together with traces of iron objects. Finds of weaving tools and loom weights indicate that cloth production was prevalent later in the 9th century. Pottery kilns were also found, together with the debris from metal working and quantities of bone objects, making this a commercially thriving community for over 13 centuries. An excellent source of information and detail about the excavations is Christopher Scull's book *Early medieval (late 5th-early 8th centuries AD) Cemeteries at Boss Hall and Buttermarket Ipswich Suffolk* (2009).

The friary associated with the cemetery (although the burials took place outside the settlement itself) is that of the Carmelite Order of Whitefriars which stood south of the Buttermarket and extended from Queen Street to St Stephen's Lane. It was the largest religious community in Ipswich and one of the largest Carmelite House in England. The friars' white cloaks, worn over a brown habit, gave them the name Whitefriars.

The friary was founded in 1278, though by whom is not clear as there were several patrons including Sir Thomas de Loudham and Sir Jeffrey Hadley. Edward I visited Ipswich in 1277 and later bestowed benefits on the Order. Ipswich Whitefriars attracted a larger number of eminent scholars than did the other friaries and supplied several provincial superiors to the Order. It often hosted meetings of the Order's provincial chapters so it was no wonder that the site came to extend over a large area. Such was the influence of the Order that Ipswich was the first to begin a women's section. In 1400 an Ipswich woman named Agnes was admitted to their ranks, founding what subsequently became known as the Institute of Recluses.

Henry VI and his court were entertained at the friary in 1452.

The dissolution of the priory in 1538 was conducted by Thomas Cromwell (Walk 4). By then it had become an impoverished community, having to sell pieces of land to raise enough money to survive. A few buildings which once formed part of Whitefriars survived into the 19th century but they have long since disappeared from view.

One of the most famous priors of the Ipswich Carmelites was the last elected before the dissolution, John Bale (1495–1563) whose career was, to say the very least, colourful. He was known as 'Bilious Bale' by contemporary scholars due to his 'earthy' turn of phrase and 'his rude vigour of expression and his want of good taste and moderation'. Having taken monastic vows he later renounced them in favour of marriage (and several children) and managed to tread a religious tightrope by switching from Catholicism to Protestantism and later back again to Catholicism. Having occasioned considerable scandal by advising his fellow priests to marry, he was sent by Edward VI to Ireland, an uninspired move since most of the clergy there remained faithful to Catholicism and clerical chastity.

Among his many literary works is a play entitled *Kynge Johan* (King John) written in 1538 which marks a transition from the old morality plays to English historical drama. The original manuscript was discovered in the 1830s in the Ipswich Borough archives where there were also references to charitable foundations by King John in the town (Walk 2).

**Opposite the Buttermarket Shopping Centre is St Stephen's Church which houses the TIC.**

There was a church here at Domesday though the building of St Stephen's seen today is a mix of 15th and 16th-century architecture and has been restored many times. It was declared redundant in 1975 and for 20 years was in the doldrums until transformed into the Tourist Information Centre in 1994.

*St Stephen's Lane goes south from the TIC.*

*St Stephen's Church is now the TIC.*

*The Buttermarket Shopping Centre entrance is opposite the TIC.*

Before leaving, notice a monument in the chancel to Robert and Mary Leman who died on the same day in 1637.

Part of the church's former environs can still be seen and the resting places in what was the old churchyard offer a place to sit and relax. There is a convenient seating area in Arras Square, a vantage point where St Stephen's church faces the Buttermarket Shopping Centre.

The Buttermarket Shopping Centre was built in 1992 and has both lift and stair access.

**Walk south along St Stephen's Lane towards the Old Cattle Market.**

A short way down (on the left-hand side) is the Old Sun Inn which dates from the 16th century (or before) but with the usual additions and alterations made over subsequent years. A lane once ran alongside the Sun Inn (west-to-east) and, if the gates are open, you can see a line of setts (broken stones) in the courtyard. There are only two places in the town where setts can still be seen: one is here and the other is in Coytes Gardens (Walk 4).

Formerly known as the Rising Sun, it is tempting to associate the inn with Edward III who was frequently in Ipswich. He spent time in the town during 1338–40 (when he conferred a confirmatory charter on the town) and his badge was a rising sun, a symbol of optimism (Walk 8).

The sun rising over the sea is, incidentally, the main charge in the Suffolk Coat of Arms and was used as the badge of Suffolk at the battle of Agincourt in 1415.

*The courtyard of the Old Sun Inn a short way down St Stephen's.*

Between 1810 and 1897 the Provision Market was held in the vicinity of the Old Cattle Market opposite Silent Street.

St Stephen's Lane becomes Turret Lane as it continues southward, across the bus station. The two lanes form one of the oldest continuous thoroughfares in Ipswich that linked the town markets with the port. It also once led to one of the entrances of the Priory of St Peter and St Paul (Walk 7).

**Opposite the Old Cattle Market – go left on Dogs Head Street and continue until you reach the fourways junction and turn right into Lower Brook Street.**

Brook Street (divided into Upper Brook Street and Lower Brook Street) is another of the ancient north-to-south routes of the Saxon town. A cross, known as Lewes Crouch, once stood at the junction with Tacket Street and Dogs Head Street, causing Lower Brook Street to be described as 'the highway from Lewes Crouch towards the quay'.

Almost immediately the character of Lower Brook Street becomes clear. It was, in the 19th century, the home of the professional classes and nicknamed 'The Faculty'.

Halfway down on the left-hand side is The Master's House sporting a blue plaque to commemorate the physician William King (1786–1863), who was born in the house when his father, the Revd John King, was Master of Ipswich School (Walk 3).

The Revd John King was Master from 1767 to 1798: during his time at the house he provided accommodation for about 70 boarders. On his retirement he burnt the entire records of the school for which, so far, no one has been able to offer an explanation.

The house was previously called The Preacher's House, in which resided the famous town preacher Revd Samuel Ward (1577–1640) who lived there until his death. Ward was a staunch Puritan and was appointed in 1603 by the Corporation of Ipswich whose members shared his principles (Ipswich

*Master's House on Lower Brook Street once the home of the physician, William King.*

was a Puritan stronghold throughout the 17th century). He held the pulpit of St Mary le Tower for some 30 years and attracted the wrath of Archbishop Laud on more than one occasion. One of the most serious problems to beset the Archbishop was the growth of the Lecture Movement during the 1620s and 30s. Ward's weekly lectures were deemed to 'undermine the hierarchical principle' which, of course, was the point. Puritans were radical Protestants who thought that the religious reforms of Elizabeth I should have gone further and who were eager to promote more purity of religious observance. Emphasis was placed on long sermons and the reading of theological works, all designed to rid mankind of its sinful ways. Some of Samuel Ward's sermons were very long indeed and the townspeople were expected to attend, their business suspended for the duration.

Samuel Ward was the brother of Nathaniel Ward (1578–1652), another ardent Puritan who in 1634 emigrated to the Massachusetts Bay Colony in the New World. He became a minister in the town of Ipswich (founded in 1630 by John Winthrop the Younger) where he wrote *The Body of Liberties*, the first code of laws established in New England. His code was based on the fundamental principles of Common Law, the Magna Carta and the Old Testament. Ward's code led directly to the American tradition of liberty and eventually to the United States Constitution.

Ipswich (Massachusetts, USA) was originally called Agawam but in 1634 was incorporated as Ipswich, named after the town from which many of the prominent early settlers had set sail for the New World. There is a frieze commemorating their departure on the Waterfront (Walk 7).

**Continue down Lower Brook Street.**

On the right-hand side are the offices of the *East Anglian Daily Times* (*EADT*), the *Ipswich Evening Star* and other Archant titles.

The site was previously occupied by Felix Porter's Leather Factory and was where, in 1928, the Ipswich Magic Circle was founded. Felix Porter was a ventriloquist and founder member of the Magic Circle.

The *EADT* moved here in 1966 prior to the redevelopment of its Carr Street premises where it had been since 1887. The first issue was in 1874 and was at first in direct competition with the *Ipswich Journal*. Although the *Ipswich Journal* was founded in 1720, making it one of the earliest newspapers in Britain, it was published weekly, not daily. However, it did publish daily for one week in 1867 in order to lay claim to being the first daily newspaper in Suffolk. It kept going under various titles until 1902. Today the *EADT* continues as the county's only daily newspaper.

The *Ipswich Evening Star* was launched in 1884 as *The Star of the East* which did not please the publishers of the *Ipswich Journal* who introduced their own (unsuccessful) equivalent, the *Ipswich Herald*.

Opposite the Archant offices are houses built in what in the 1850s was a new style of architecture. They have four storeys and some are fronted with white Woolpit bricks which were more expensive than the ordinary red ones. It soon became common practice to have a white-brick façade on an otherwise red-brick house to give the impression of wealth.

**At the south end of Lower Brook Street turn sharp left into Foundation Street.**

A short way up Foundation Street on the left-hand side is the Ipswich Society Blue Plaque to the renowned artist, Thomas Gainsborough (1727–1788). He was born in Sudbury and in 1752 moved his wife and two daughters to Ipswich where he lived for seven years. He rented Number 34 Foundation Street (demolished in the early 1960s), a house similar to Number 32 where the plaque is mounted. His work at the time was mainly portraits and half-lengths, although he also painted small portrait groups in landscape settings. His first patron was Thomas Fonnereau, son of Claude Fonnereau of Christchurch Mansion (Walk 3) and the Member of Parliament for Sudbury.

Gainsborough was very sociable and took an active part in town life, becoming an enthusiastic member of the Ipswich Music Club, whose

*Blue Plaque to Gainsborough on Foundation Street marks the great painter's residence while in Ipswich.*

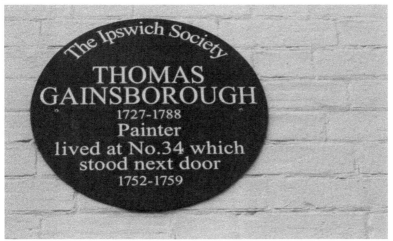

meetings were held in the Waggon and Horses Inn that once stood next to the Ancient House in the Buttermarket (Walk 2). He formed close friendships with the Town Clerk, Samuel Kilderbee, Joshua Kirby (son of John Kirby, topographer and author of *The Suffolk Traveller*) and William Craighton, publisher of the *Ipswich Journal*. He was also very great friends with the Coyte family (Walk 2) and David Garrick (see below).

Although demand for Gainsborough's work had increased on his move to Ipswich, he was persuaded that it would be even greater in Bath. Commissions came mainly from local merchants and squires but in Bath, he was told, resided a better paying high society clientele. Gainsborough and his family left Ipswich in 1759.

Opposite stands Tooleys Court, consisting of almshouses provided for in the will of Henry Tooley, a wealthy town merchant who traded with the Low Countries, Iceland and the Bay of Biscay ports (Walk 7). By about 1520 Tooley was established as a leading ship owner in the port and by his death in 1551 he had amassed a considerable fortune. He married Alice Purpet of Ipswich but, although they had three children, a son and two daughters, none survived beyond adolescence.

Another wealthy portman William Smart (whose memorial is in St Mary le Tower church, Walk 2) made endowments to the town almshouses and at his death left several bequests for the purpose of maintaining sundry poor

*Entrance to the Foundation Street almshouses.*

*Tribute to William Smart on the Foundation Street almshouses.*

*A friar from the Order of Preachers, detail from the notice board.*

persons and funding them in clothes, coals, etc. This was added to other endowments and administered by Tooley's Foundation.

Just off Foundation Street, to the right, are the excavated remains of the Dominican Friary of the Blessed Virgin, founded here by Henry III, who purchased the house of Hugh de Langeston for them in 1263. These are the only surviving relics of the pre-Reformation era when Ipswich had five religious houses. The sight of the friars in black cloak over a

*Information boards stand close by the Blackfriars ruins.*

white habit (giving them the name Blackfriars) was a familiar one in the town between the 12th and mid-16th century. The Dominicans were international brotherhoods of individuals whose members were itinerant preachers. They were known as the Order of Preachers, or Friars Preachers. Their great church here measured 177ft (54m) long and 50ft (15m) wide at the nave.

At the Dissolution several of the friary buildings were put to other uses and so survived for a time. In 1569 the Borough purchased the site to set up Christ's Hospital as a 'hospital of poor people'. The very young and the aged homeless were housed. In time it transmogrified into an infirmary, pauper school and a workhouse.

In the run up to the Civil War parts of it were converted for use as an arsenal and used to house gunpowder.

An outline history and guide to the ruins is found on the information boards on Foundation Street and beside the arcade seats in the ruins themselves. A little way past the seats, along the path leading to the junction of Fore Street and Lower Orwell Street, is a small hump of grass. This is the only remaining part of the ancient town ramparts (Walk 3).

**At the top of Foundation Street is Orwell Place to the right.**

The building on the corner of Foundation Street and Orwell Place is Unicorn House, fashioned from Catchpoles Unicorn Brewery which closed in 1923. It was used as a bottling plant for mineral waters and cordials for many years.

Orwell Place once rejoiced in the interesting and poetic name Stepples Street (from its raised stepping stones) but early in the 19th century it was renamed, unfortunately betraying a certain lack of imagination. Further down another street naming opportunity was lost: a particular stretch of Orwell Street was known in Elizabethan times as Gunpowder Lane, gaining its name from the gunpowder mill established there in 1587 by John Pavis.

This being Ipswich there is another, more earthy, explanation for Gunpowder Lane. The lower end of the street was where a stream (or wash, and at one time the northern stretch was known as The Wash) ran beside a bank which the men of the town used to relieve themselves. Over the years the ground became so inundated with sulphur that the earth was later treated and used to make gunpowder!

**From Orwell Place, turn left onto Tacket Street and almost immediately is Cox Lane on the right-hand side.**

Cox Lane runs alongside the red brick St Pancras Roman Catholic Chapel and into the car park.

Catholicism was re-established in the town after a refugee priest, Pere Louis Pierre Simon (died 1839), fled the terrors of the French Revolution. He was given shelter by a Catholic woman living in Silent Street, Mrs Margaret Wood, and remained a priest in Ipswich for 46 years. Pere Simon extended his ministry to include the Irish Catholics among the 8,000 soldiers who were stationed in the town during the Napoleonic Wars.

St Pancras was built in 1861 and opened by the Bishop of Northampton. Monsignor Henry Manning, who later became head of the Catholic Church in England as Cardinal Manning, preached the sermon.

Over the next few years anti-Catholic riots took place in the town, causing the clergy to barricade themselves in their homes for days on end. Catholic-owned businesses and houses were stoned and the mayor had to enrol 200 special constables to restore order.

Inside the church is a shrine to Our Lady of Poland, a memorial to members of the Polish Free Armies who stayed in the town during World War Two. It was presented by the crew of the Polish C Armoured Train and is cared for by the local Polish community.

When Mother Theresa visited Ipswich in 1970 she was welcomed by the then Parish Priest of St Pancras, Fr Norman Smith.

Further along on the right-hand side is a reminder of the strong links with non-conformity that have always existed in the town. Now called Christ Church, it is an inter-denominational fellowship which comprises

*Christ Church in the spring.*

Tacket Street United Reformed Church (formerly Congregational), founded in 1686, and Turret Green Baptist Church, founded in 1842. It opened in 1720, built in the Gothic revival style and designed by the noted Ipswich architect, Frederick Barnes.

One of the first ministers of the new Meeting House was Revd William Notcutt (minister from 1724–56) who came from Somerset, the first of the famous family of gardeners who founded the Notcutts Garden Centres.

Another early minister was the Revd William Gordon (later Revd Dr Gordon), who came to Christ Church in 1754. He went to America to support the cause of American Independence as a result of which the British government placed a price on his head. However, when peace was declared he was allowed to return to England and died in Ipswich in 1807. He is buried in the churchyard.

William Gordon worked closely with the first American President, George Washington (1732–99), who in 1783 wrote to William Gordon saying that unless adequate powers were given to Congress for the purposes of a Federal Union 'we shall soon moulder into dust and become contemptible in the eyes of Europe'.

In 1788 William Gordon published the first history of the Revolution in four volumes, *History of the Rise, Progress and Establishment of the Independence of the United States of America.*

In 1795, the year that the London Missionary Society was founded, a member of the congregation, Daniel Bowell (1774–99), volunteered for the missions. In 1796 he sailed for the island of Tongataboo, one of the Tahitian islands of the Pacific. He survived only three years. In 1799 Daniel and two other missionaries were caught up in a civil war and were 'barbarously murdered'.

The area surrounding Cox Lane and Upper Orwell Street is associated with the mint that operated here from the 10th to the late 13th century. The area is now referred to as the Mint Quarter and includes Tacket Street and Carr Street, the name taking over from its earlier label The Cloisters, which appeared in a development plan dating back to the early 1990s.

King Edgar set up a Royal Mint in *Gipeswic* in 937. The earliest names we have of town inhabitants are Leofric and Liginge, moneyers at the Ipswich Mint. A silver coin dating from Edgar's reign has *Gipswic* on it, providing the earliest version of the town name.

In 2010 a rare example of an Anglo-Saxon penny of King Edward the Martyr (died 978) went under the hammer and was sold for £10,000. It was minted in Ipswich in the 10th century and was one of only five known examples of the coin in Europe.

Cox Lane has recently been suggested as the site of a rare mediaeval Fortified Town House. Defended town houses are recorded in historic documents as being surrounded by a substantial ditch, as was found here.

### Proceed along Tacket Street.

A short way past Christ Church is Wingfield Street, a reminder of another prominent man in Tudor Ipswich, Sir Humphry Wingfield (died 1545), Speaker in the House of Commons, who lived hereabouts. His first appearance at court was in the household of Mary, Dowager Queen of France and sister of Henry VIII. She had married Sir Charles Brandon in France against her brother's wishes and it was Sir Humphry who assisted the pair to 'lie low' in Suffolk until the king had been placated. It is said that the couple took a house on Upper Brook Street before taking up residence at Westhorpe Hall in West Suffolk.

Some years later, in 1553, Sir Humphry played host to Queen Mary as she made her way from Framlingham Castle to London to claim the throne.

Sir Humphry's nephew, Sir Anthony Wingfield, Knight of the Garter and Vice-Chamberlain to Henry VIII, also had a house in Ipswich, Brooks Hall. Sir Anthony served at the Battle of the Spurs in 1513 and was knighted for his part in the capture of Tournai (Belgium). A few years later he accompanied the King to the Field of the Cloth of Gold, an extravagant diplomatic spectacle staged in France by Henry and Francis I of France and masterminded by fellow Ipswichian, Thomas Wolsey.

Wingfield House was on the north side of Tacket Street, an area currently being used as a temporary car park. The mid-18th century saw the grand Tudor houses of Ipswich fall into decay and by 1764 Wingfield House had became the Tankard Inn, the chapel having previously been converted into The Tacket Street Playhouse. It was here that a then unknown actor named David Garrick (1716–79) made his professional debut in 1741 as Aboan, the African slave in Thomas Southerne's tragedy *Oroonoko*. He wished to appear 'under the disguise of a black countenance' in case his nervous attempts at acting should fail. The Ipswich audience afforded him huge applause and he went on to enjoy a 30-year career as one of the most influential figures in British theatre history.

The Tacket Street Playhouse attracted the county's 'gentlefolk', and it was also popular with those who attended the Ipswich Races (Walk 2). The various troupes of travelling players were popular, especially with officers from the local garrison. On one occasion, when the theatre was very busy, there were no seats available for the officers so they shouted 'Fire!' and started a near fatal panic.

*View down Tacket Street from Upper Brook Street.*

Although nothing of Wingfield House remains the interior panelling of the very grand room in which the two Tudor queens – Mary, Dowager Queen of France (sister of Henry VIII) and Queen Mary – were entertained can be seen at Christchurch Mansion (Walk 3). The Wingfield Room arrived there by a circuitous route, being acquired by Christchurch Museum in 1929.

Tacket Street finishes at the four-ways intersection between Upper and Lower Brook Street and becomes Dogs Head Street (see Walk 4).

**To return to the TIC continue along Dogs Head Street and turn right into St Stephen's Lane.**

To reach the town centre continue northwards up St Stephen's Lane. Before you leave Arras Square, created when the Buttermarket Shopping Centre was built, notice the yellow post box from Arras inside the centre immediately opposite

*Post box from Arras in the Buttermarket Shopping Centre (TIC in background).*

*The entrance to the TIC in Arras Square.*

St Stephen's church. The square is named for the town of Arras in Pas de Calais in the north of France, with which Ipswich was first 'twinned' in 1993. In 2003 a new charter was signed between the two communities agreeing to jointly promote education, cultural, sporting and social exchanges.

# WALK 6

# ITFC AND THE RIVERSIDE WALK

Walk 6 is a circular walk which starts and finishes at Ipswich Railway Station, taking in:

*Railway Station – Princes Street – Riverside Walk – West End Road – Chancery Road – Russell Road – Endeavour House – Grafton House – Constantine Road – Alf Ramsey Way – Portman Road – Ipswich Town Football Club – Grafton Way – Cardinal Park – Stoke Bridge – Riverside Walk – Railway Station*

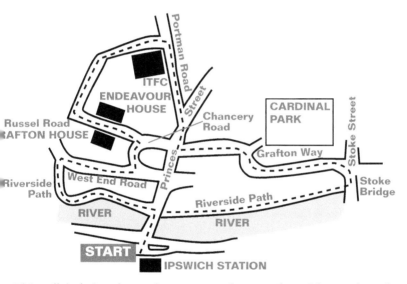

This walk is designed to explore an unusual aspect of Ipswich away from the town centre, giving walkers an opportunity to discover the banks of the River Orwell. Be aware that the riverside path runs immediately along the river bank. It becomes narrower at various points and there are no safety rails.

In addition to the football stadium there is an opportunity to see modern architecture in the judicial and administrative centres. Ipswich is proud of its plentiful town artworks and many of them are found on this walk. In spite of the modernity of its buildings, this part of the town nevertheless has its roots firmly in its long and distinguished heritage. Cardinal Park is the first refreshment opportunity apart from the railway station, which has a buffet restaurant, shop and some vending machines on the platforms.

The railway was late coming to Suffolk. Although the line from London to Colchester was laid by 1823, it took another 23 years to reach Ipswich. For centuries the town had looked to the sea for its trade, prosperity and links with the wider world, while the late 18th century had opened up road travel for both business and pleasure with improved access to and from London. Good communications beyond the River Orwell had been the basis for the town's prosperity. The additional possibilities opened up by rail links gave Ipswich another lease of life.

Credit for the eventual opening of the railway was due almost entirely to John Chevallier Cobbold, MP for the borough and family member of town benefactors (Walk 3). John Cobbold and a cohort of local entrepreneurs and philanthropists realised that unless Ipswich joined the rail network the entire county would suffer and Ipswich be reduced to a backwater town.

A new company was set up, the Eastern Union Railway Company, and the line was duly extended from Colchester to Ipswich. When it was opened on 11 June 1846 the mayor declared a town holiday and 600 ladies welcomed the first train, waving 'snowy kerchiefs'.

One of the problems with bringing the railway to Ipswich was the river. The first station was in Croft Street, south of the river in Stoke parish. When another line was suggested, linking Ipswich to Bury St Edmunds, it was proposed to connect the two lines by a viaduct.

The hero of the hour was civil engineer Peter Schuyler Bruff (1812–1900) who was justifiably called 'the Brunel of the Eastern Counties'. Bruff had worked for the Eastern Counties Railway in the early 1840s on building a rail link between Shoreditch and Colchester. He suggested that rather than a viaduct a tunnel should be excavated through Stoke Hill.

The resulting tunnel is considered by railway connoisseurs to be a superb feat of engineering. It was the first such tunnel to be constructed on a continuous curve and is unique to East Anglia. The line to Bury St Edmunds was opened in 1846 and the following years an extension of the line to Norwich was started.

When Stoke Tunnel was excavated some extraordinary finds were made including remains of a rhinoceros, lion and mammoth: more about this is to be found in Ipswich Museum (Walk 1).

Employees of the railway were obliged to live in the immediate area, especially engine drivers, and many of them lived in Stoke parish. Punctuality was a by-word for the rail managers and trains had to leave on time. Consequently, in the days before reliable alarm clocks the company sent people round knocking on doors to remind them of the time, a practice that continued into the 1950s.

The station building seen today opened in 1860 at the north end of the tunnel.

*Ipswich is only 69 miles from London Liverpool Street.*

Following the advent of the railways, Ipswich had everything going for it. What could not be brought in by road or rail could still be transported by water. The improvements on the waterfront, and construction of the Wet Dock in 1842 (Walk 8), meant that the town could capitalise on the cut and thrust of Victorian enterprise and horizons broadened beyond anything that had come before.

*Ipswich Railway Station.*

*Victorian railway architecture still graces Ipswich Station.*

The Ipswich train service is currently run by National Express East Anglia.

The new footbridge and lifts were opened in 2011. Previously passengers unable to use the stairs were escorted over the tracks to platforms 3 and 4.

The full and fascinating story of Ipswich's railway history, and more about the other many and considerable achievements of Peter Bruff, is to be found at the Ipswich Transport Museum (see Useful Information and Contacts).

The Over Stoke History Group also safeguards old documents and photographs relating to Stoke and has built up a considerable archive.

*Town buses depart for the town centre from the front of the station building.*

*Princes Street bridge (ITFC in background).*

Immediately opposite the station is the Station Hotel. Its position, between the railway station and the Ipswich Town Football Club stadium 200 yards away, means that it attracts both home and away supporters. On match days, however, it becomes the away fans' pub as part of a scheme arranged with the police to ensure a safe atmosphere.

**Cross the road onto the left-hand side of Princess Street Bridge, and once over the bridge turn left onto the riverside.**

The Riverside Path (down the steps) and the Cycle Path (immediately ahead) both end at the same destination.

The Cycle Path is part of the National Cycle Route 51 and follows the route of the old docklands railway that once ran down to Greenwich.

The Riverside Walk is part of the 17-mile Gipping Valley River Path. It was formerly the Gipping Navigation tow path, along which horses would have pulled barges. In 1793–94 the Ipswich and Stowmarket Navigation venture began after many years of discussion. Ipswich Town Council had put the brakes on the scheme as the local merchants thought that trade to Stowmarket would be sent direct without paying any tolls at Ipswich. It is thought that the name shown on the authorising act for the Navigation in 1790 as 'Gipping' was chosen deliberately so as not to upset Ipswich by calling it the Orwell Navigation.

*The Sir Bobby Robson Bridge, where the old weir can still be seen at low tide.*

When it did get finally come into being, it stretched from the Orwell estuary up to Stowmarket with 15 locks rising 90ft within its length. It was not a canal but an improvement to the navigation of the natural river. Some of the coal which came into Ipswich docks was carried inland while Stowmarket's corn and malt trades improved. The scheme had taken so long to get going, however, that it prospered for not much more than 50 years and was superseded by the coming of the railways. It closed in 1922 and was abandoned 10 years later when the right of navigation was extinguished and ownership of the river reverted to the riparian owners on either side.

The river is still tidal above the Princes Street Bridge, beyond the weir seen at low tide above the Sir Bobby Robson Bridge (see below) and on up to the Handford Tide Lock and the sluice above Handford Bridge. The precise point at which the Gipping becomes the Orwell is uncertain and the cause of much discussion.

The River Gipping Trust has an excellent website (see Useful Information and Contacts) which provides up-to-date information about the work being carried out in collaboration with the Inland Waterways Association (which has seen Bosmere, Creeting and Baylham locks fully restored).

On the Cycle Path stands the 16ft-high 'corten' iron sculpture *Navigator* (2003) by John Atkin, commissioned by the River Action Group, below which is a mural facing the river.

From 1880 until the 1950s Old Cattle Yard Pocket Park (further along) was used to house cattle and other stock on its way to or from the cattle market. Herdsmen used to sleep in a disused railway carriage (now overgrown) to deal with stock that arrived on late or early trains.

Note the Sir Bobby Robson Bridge, opened in 2009, which links the Fairvew 'Voyager' Estate with Ranelagh Road, the football stadium and the town centre. The 'cable stayed' bridge spans 60m and hangs from a 35m high 'wishbone' pylon. There are eight suspension wires in four parallel pairs.

It was named after a competition was organised by the *Evening Star* and cost around £800,000 to build.

The weir north of the bridge was built in about 1903 to provide cooling water for the electricity station.

**Leaving the riverside, join West End Road and cross to the north side of the road via the pedestrian crossing a short distance away.**

Going east on West End Road the road bears round to the left into Chancery Road, where stands the imposing five-court Ipswich Crown Court building which has another commissioned art work immediately behind the glazed façade on the Chancery Road aspect. *Untitled* is by Jacqueline Poncelet (2004). For a closer look entry is allowed into the Crown Court building, but photography is not allowed. There is an attendant in the entrance hall who will advise on what is permissible and what is not.

The side rear walls are clad in stainless steel panels and gable walls in Suffolk white brick.

## Turn left into Russell Road.

Russell Road has become the administrative centre for the Ipswich Borough Council and Suffolk County Council. Grafton House (on the left) is the Ipswich Borough Council headquarters and was opened in March 2007. It houses the Council's 24–7 CCTV control room.

Grafton House was named for HMS *Grafton*, a Type-23 frigate of the Royal Navy affiliated to the Borough in 1996 which was the eighth vessel to bear the name. The first was commanded by the 27-year-old Duke of Grafton in the 17th century. The seat of the Dukes of Grafton is in Suffolk and the Duke holds the subsidiary titles of Viscount Ipswich and Baron Sudbury.

The Ship's Bell was presented to the mayor, Councillor Bill Wright, on HMS *Grafton's* last sea trip under the White Ensign in 2006, in recognition of the town's special relationship with her. On this, their last visit, the crew were

*Replica of the Ipswich Ship in Grafton House on Russell Road.*

*Lightships on the glass frontage of Grafton House: the ships were drawn by members of staff.*

awarded the Freedom of the Borough. HMS *Grafton* was decommissioned in 2004 and sold to the Chilean Navy in 2007. The bell can be seen in the reception area.

The glass frontage is the location for the 10m-long *Lightships*, a commissioned art work by Mark Dixon, installed in 2007. It is lit with ultra-bright LEDs controlled by micro-electronics. Some of the lights symbolising the surface of the sea are triggered by mobile phones and change colour during the day: at night the ships themselves are coloured. It is visible from both inside and outside the building and was inspired by the concept of communication, using the latest LED technology. The boats were drawn by the resident staff of the Borough Council.

Inside is also a model of the Ipswich Ship resembling that on the Great Seal of Ipswich. The ship is one of the first depictions of a vessel with a rudder. Other vessels at that time and before were steered by an oar hung over the quarter. The 'castles' at the ship's bow and stern are built for defence (against pirates or when converted to a warship) and the storage of water-vulnerable cargoes.

In the Middle Ages, two types of trading vessels served the East Coast, the German Cog and the Cat. The Ipswich Ship is similar to a Cog (from the German *kogge*), a ship widely used from the 10th century onward and associated with seagoing trade in mediaeval Europe, especially the

Hanseatic League (an early economic alliance for the Baltic Sea trading area), which had a representative merchant and warehousing facilities in Ipswich.

The Cats were early cargo ships and, among other things, brought coal from Newcastle along the East Coast to London and survived in some form until the end of the 17th century.

It is thought that the legends surrounding Sir Richard Whittington (*c.*1354–1423), made famous in the pantomime versions of *Dick Whittington and his Cat*, may originate from his having sailed on a Cat in the course of his business. Apprenticed to the Mercers' Company, Sir Richard was a merchant, astute politician (three times Mayor of London) and money lender to the kings of England. It is entirely possible that he came to Ipswich as a cloth merchant, specialising in silk, damask and velvet, and that the cat carved on the corner post of the Old Bell Inn (Walk 8) is a reference to the Cat vessels.

A replica of a Cat ship is incorporated into the second panel of the Charter Wall Hangings which can be seen in St Peter's Church (Walk 7). An impression of the original seal is kept in the Mayor's Parlour at the town hall.

Daniel Defoe, in his history of the Great Plague, writes that the 'dreadful malady' was carried to Ipswich 'by those large vessels called the Ipswich Cats'.

Opposite stands Endeavour House, the Suffolk County Council Headquarters. The Council bought the partially-completed building in 2003,

*View of Endeavour House through the* Lightships *of Grafton House.*

*The shuttle bus leaves from the Suffolk County Council headquarters, Endeavour House on Russell Road.*

and it opened for business the following year. It was originally built to house the TXU Energy offices. It is open-plan with glass walls both inside and out, which takes advantage of natural light. Three wings are built round a central atrium with staircases and bridges linking all areas.

In the lobby are eight large outline icons of Suffolk – a pylon, bridge, pumping station, Scot's Pine, street light and the Barking Tye water tower. There is a key to the icons, which were commissioned by TXU Energy, on the front of the reception desk.

The building takes its name from Suffolk County Council's motto: Guide Our Endeavour.

A free shuttle bus into town leaves from the front of Endeavour House.

**Continue along Russell Road, and turn right onto Constantine Road and right again onto Sir Alf Ramsey Way.**

There is a deceptively open space here at the junction in front of the play area: the bus depot is on the corner of Constantine Road and care should be taken at busy times of the day.

Immediately ahead is the Alderman Road Recreation Ground and play area, the Ipswich Town Football Club (ITFC) stadium is on the right. Seating

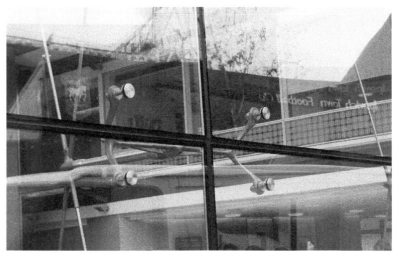

*ITFC logo reflected onto the glass of Endeavour House.*

capacity of just over 30,000 with four stands – the Cobbold, South, Britannia and Sir Bobby Robson stands.

Ipswich Town FC started as an amateur club (called the Ipswich Association Football Club to distinguish it from the local rugby club) in 1878 and moved to Portman Road in 1888, initially sharing the ground with the rugby club and East Suffolk Cricket Club.

During World War One the pitch was requisitioned by the army and when peace returned the ground was in a sorry state. Money was badly needed so the club opened its doors to whippet racing and a groundsman – who kept chickens, goats and sheep in one of the stands – was brought in to effect repairs to the turf.

In 1936 a second team was formed, called Ipswich United, which threatened to put on rival matches at the Greyhound Stadium. After pressure from supporters, a meeting was called at the town hall on 1 May 1936 when it was agreed that the team would turn professional, starting in the Third (Southern) Division. They were elected to the Football League by a margin of just two votes. Blue and white were adopted as the official club colours from the outset.

The club's first professional game at Portman Road was against Tunbridge Wells Rangers, which the home side won 4–1. They caused a footballing sensation by winning the Championship of the Southern League in their first season, without losing an away match. The team attracted the attention of A. Scott Duncan, then manager of Manchester United, who became secretary-manager of the club in their second season.

In World War Two the ground escaped damage from enemy action, but the club closed down for the duration.

Over the years, Ipswich Town FC has enjoyed a strong and loyal following. There are currently 27 branches of the Ipswich Town Supporters' Club serving Town fans all around the world.

In 1990 for the first time in the history of the club the football stadium was used as a rock venue, with Tina Turner the star turn. The pitch was specially covered for the event.

Fixture lists can be found on the ITFC website (details in Useful Information and Contacts).

Walking along Alf Ramsey Way, you come to the life-size bronze statue of Sir Alfred Ramsey (1920–99) on the left-hand side junction with Portman Road. Sculpted by Sean Hedges-Quinn in 2000, it was unveiled by former Ipswich striker Ray Crawford, who played for Ipswich from 1958 until 1963.

Sir Alf was ITFC manager from 1955 to 1963, during which time he led the team to the Division One 1961–62 Championship title (under the captaincy of Andy Nelson), just a year after having won the Division Two Championship. In 1963 he was appointed manager of the England football team and led the national side to glory in the 1966 World Cup at Wembley. He was knighted in 1967 and continued to live in Ipswich until his death in 1999.

**Turn right along Portman Road.**

The name Portman Road comes from the 13th-century town portmen who were elected following King John's Charter, given to the town in 1200 (Walk 2). The 12 portmen were allowed to graze their horses on a marsh meadow called Oldenholm. In time it became known as Portmen's Marsh and for many years Sir Alf Ramsey Way was known as Portman's Walks, as this was their route from the town to the marshes, part of which is now occupied by the ITFC complex.

For better or worse, the 13th-century office of portman continued until 1835 when the Municipal Reform Act of that year changed the Borough officers to mayor, aldermen and councillors.

Changes to the road configurations were made during the Victorian development of the railway station and the creation of Princes Street (Walk 4) and altered again in the 1980s when new traffic schemes were introduced.

A few yards along Portman Road is the statue of another football and town hero, Sir Robert William 'Bobby' Robson CBE (1933–2009) who managed ITC from 1969 to 1982 and guided them to victory in the FA Cup and UEFA

*'Sir Alf' on Portman Road.*

*Sir Bobby continues to inspire and remains a town hero.*

Cup before being appointed England manager in 1982. The sculpture was commissioned by the Ipswich Town Supporters' Association and funded by Ipswich Borough Council and TXU.

Sir Bobby was a town and football hero of no mean proportion. His 'dignified and gentlemanly' personality was said to transcend the game: he was called a 'footballing colossus'. His motto was said to have been 'love the game more than the prize' and he was held in high affection and respect in and outside the game.

In 2006 Sir Bobby (knighted in 2002) was named as honorary president of Ipswich Town Football Club, the first since Lady Blanche Cobbold who had died in 1987. In May 2008 he visited the town to celebrate the 30th anniversary of the club's FA Cup victory and was awarded the Freedom of the Borough of Ipswich.

After Sir Bobby was diagnosed as suffering from cancer he began raising funds for the early detection of cancer and a foundation was set up in his name. Following his death in July 2009, thousands of shirts and scarves were laid in tribute at his statue. The following Saturday, the North Stand was officially renamed the Sir Bobby Robson Stand. More than 27,000 fans, ex-players and dignitaries of both Ipswich Town and Newcastle United took part in celebrations of Sir Bobby's life.

In September 2009 Cornhill was packed as people flocked to watch the live broadcast of Sir Bobby's Memorial Service from Durham Cathedral.

*View of the Princes Street bridge from the Riverside Walk.*

*Sir Bobby Robson statue on Portman Road.*

*The* Navigator *by John Atkin along the eastern side of the Riverside Walk.*

**Continue southwards on Portman Road to rejoin Princes Street.**

To return to the railway station, continue back down Princes Street and back over the bridge (the station is seen straight ahead).

*The Stoke Bridge start of the Riverside Walk which leads to the railway station.*

*Stoke Bridge with St Mary at Stoke tower in the background.*

To reach the town centre, turn left on Princes Street and keep walking until you reach Giles Circus.

For a longer walk, thus returning to the station via another section of the Riverside Walk, turn left on Grafton Way and carry on past Quadling Street. Unfortunately, this does go beside a very busy road but there are wide pavements and several crossing places.

To the left is Cardinal Leisure Park, which is the first refreshment opportunity on this walk (apart from the railway station which has a buffet restaurant).

Cardinal Park was created in 1998–99 as a major development based on entertainment and leisure. There are bars, a Gym & Trim health club and Cineworld (on Grafton Way). It derives its name from Cardinal Wolsey, whose college was intended to have been close to St Peter's Church (Walks 4 and 7) had it been completed.

Notice that seven of the carved granite bollards (by Bettina Furnee, 1996) are engraved with lines from films. The bollards function as part of the local traffic scheme.

**Continue along Grafton Way and use the pedestrian crossings to reach Stoke Bridge.**

From here the Waterfront is easily accessible via the crossing places on the bridge, and there are plenty of cafés and restaurants along the quaysides (Walk 8).

To return to the station rejoin the Riverside Walk at River Park. Look for the start of the path near the bronze and iron sculpture *Against the Tide* by Laurence Edwards (2004) next to the skateboard park. It is easy to spot as it is sited on the top of a tall concrete plinth marked 'River Path'.

A few yards along the Riverside Walk, close to Stoke Bridge (Walk 8), the mediaeval parish Church of St Mary at Stoke can be seen on the opposite bank.

Stairs leading up to Princes Street are found after passing under the bridge.

Town buses depart from several stops in front of the railway station. There is an information poster in the main bus stand.

# WALK 7

## THE FIVE CHURCHES

Walk 7 is a circular walk starting at University College Suffolk (UCS) and finishing on the Waterfront, taking in:

*UCS – Neptune Quay – Coprolite Street – Duke Street – St Clement's Congregational Church – Back Hamlet – Fore Street – Holy Trinity Church – Grimwade Street – Suffolk New College – Neptune Square – St Clement's Church Lane – St Clement's Church – Salthouse Street – Key Street – St Mary at Quay Church – College Street – St Peter's Church – Stoke Street – Waterfront*

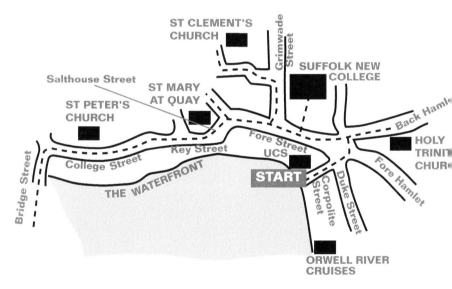

This walk concentrates on the five churches in the Waterfront area and involves quite a bit of pavement walking some of it beside very busy streets. The traffic is continuous along College and Key Street, but there is regrettably no other way to reach St Mary at Quay. There are numerous places of rest and recuperation along the Waterfront.

UCS is accessed from the nearby visitors' car park, by bus from Tower Ramparts (see Town Transport) or on foot from the town centre.

*Neptune Quay on the north of the Wet Dock.*

The walk begins from the UCS (Walk 8), turning into Coprolite Street along the eastern curve of the main building.

Coprolite Street is a small link road between Neptune Quay and Duke Street, but its name recalls the advent of artificial fertilizer, Professor J.S. Henslow of Hitcham (Professor Botany at Cambridge University and mentor to Charles Darwin) and the glory days of Ipswich docks in the 19th century.

Coprolite (fossil dung) had been used to improve crops since 1718, but it was Henslow who discovered that the phosphoric value of the coprolite nodules would have a more concentrated effect if it was extracted, ground up and treated with sulphuric acid, instead of being left on the land to disintegrate of its own volition.

Edward Packard began grinding coprolite nuggets in his mill at Snape (on the River Alde) in 1843 and before long he was producing super phosphates which were to revolutionise farming methods for all time.

*University College Suffolk building is prominent on the Waterfront.*

*Waterfront with St Mary at Quay tower in background.*

Between the 1840s and 1890s the trade flourished, with barges bringing coprolite to Ipswich Docks, laying the foundation of a later fertiliser industry. Coprolite mining began on an industrial scale and before long other companies joined in so that by 1880 there were five firms manufacturing artificial fertilizer, among them William Colchester, Joseph Fison and Company, Edward Packard and Prentice Brothers. In 1929, three of these were united as Fison, Packard and Prentice, which was to morph into the internationally known Fisons Limited.

'Edward Fison Ltd' can still be seen at the end of a building on the upper reaches of the East Cut on the Stoke side of the bridge. It is visible from the colonnades just before The Mill (see below).

**Take the Duke Street pedestrian crossings across what used to be called the Duke Street Roundabout (to be re-named the Duke Street Public Realm) and turn right into Back Hamlet – Holy Trinity Church is on the right-hand side.**

That Ipswich still has 12 mediaeval churches (seven of them existing at Domesday) is well known, but the second church on this walk has only recently been highlighted as one of the town's rare gems of a later date.

Holy Trinity Church was built as Chapel of Ease to St Clement's Church (see below) and opened in 1835 on rising ground above Fore Hamlet. It is one of the few churches in England to be built during the reign of William IV

*One of the two roundels in Holy Trinity Church.*

(1830–37) and one of the first Anglican churches to have been built in Ipswich since the Reformation. Its understated exterior belies its Georgian Baroque interior.

The church is usually open to visitors during the day and the church guide gives its history. Notice in particular the two roundels in the west window which represent the two seals of the pre-Reformation Priory of the Holy Trinity (now Christchurch Mansion, see Walk 3). They have been placed here as a reminder of the pre-Reformation Priory of Christchurch (Holy Trinity and Christ Church were then interchangeable) which stood on the site of Christchurch Mansion (Walk 3). Opinions vary as to their precise age.

The first seal represents Christ seated on a throne, in each corner the mystic emblems of the four evangelists, Matthew, Mark, Luke and John. The text reads Seal of Christ Church Ipswich. The second seal depicts the Lamb with the standard of the Cross.

**Returning to Back Hamlet going towards Fore Street, you pass the St Clement's Congregational Church on the right.**

Where Back Hamlet meets the Duke Street Realm, on the right-hand side is the second church, St Clement's Congregational Church, which stands opposite the Grimwade Memorial Hall now converted into loft-style apartments. The hall was built in 1869 as a chapel but, when the congregation expanded, the new church was built on the other side of the road.

The red-brick Victorian Congregational Church was built in 1887 and takes the name 'St Clement' because of its parish, not as a dedication. It was built by the Grimwade family in memory of Edward Grimwade (see below) who had died in 1886.

**To access Suffolk New College (via walkway), return to the Duke Street Realm onto Fore Street and go north across Waterfront visitors' car park, at the top of which is a walkway.**

Suffolk New College took four years to build and was opened in February 2010 by the England football manager, Fabio Capello. The higher education provision previously held by (the old) Suffolk College was transferred to UCS in 2007. Suffolk New College now concentrates on Further Education, vocational programmes and apprenticeships.

It is worth seeing one of the town's modern architectural giants, complete with Reglit glass. There is a café in the brightly-coloured atrium.

Nearby is a Goals Soccer Centre.

*Walkway from the Waterfront car park to Suffolk New College.*

*Suffolk New College was named as winner of the Archant Suffolk Business Awards 2010 for Diversity.*

**Return to Fore Street via the walkway and then across the car park.**

Immediately ahead, next to the UCS building, is a small row of what, until around 1895, were cottages. A carved bressumer beam at first-floor level bears the date 1620.

**Turn right and proceed along Fore Street, turning right into Grimwade Street.**

Grimwade Street is named after Alderman Edward Grimwade, a member of one of the town's illustrious families. J.H. Grimwade & Sons had premises which operated on Cornhill from 1844 until 1996, their red brick establishment being on the corner of Cornhill and Westgate Street.

In Grimwade Street is a terrace of four houses called the Captains Houses along which a richly carved bressumer beam, dated 1631, runs between Number 79 and 83. It is thought to be the longest in the country. The houses are reputed to have been home to 176 sea captains over the years.

**A short way up Grimwade Street turn left into St Clements Church Lane.**

The third church of the walk is in St Clements Church Lane which leads to one of the three mediaeval churches in the Waterfront area. They stand in close proximity to minister to the crowded neighbourhoods of their time. The apostrophe in Clement's is invariably omitted.

St Clement's was erected in about 1500 on earlier foundations and was known as the Sailors' Church because of the strong and enduring links with seafarers. Even the name is a reminder of the sea: St Clement is the patron saint of sailors and seamen and his emblem, an anchor, appears in a stone shield above the western belfry window.

Ship building has taken place along one or other of the Ipswich quays beside the River Orwell from the 13th century right up to the modern day. Ships of varying design and size were built here over the centuries and the last of the old yards to be closed was Dock End in the early 1970s.

The earliest vessel known to have been built in an Ipswich shipyard, probably in St Clement's parish, was in 1294–95 when a galley was commissioned by Edward I. One of the builders was Philip Harneys whose yard was at Ding Quay. The town bailiffs John of Causton and John Lew rendered the account to the Exchequer at a cost of £195 4s 11p, which included the wages of a master carpenter and shipwrights for 21 weeks and

*St Clement's Church is a haven of quiet in a busy part of town.*

1 day. There were additional charges for repair to the galley after she had been damaged in a storm while on trials in the Thames Estuary.

In 1588 Ipswich built, fitted out and manned two ships to sail against the Spanish Armada.

The *Ardwina* is thought to have been the last of the Thames sailing barges to be built in Ipswich and she was launched from St Clement's Yard in 1909. For much of her working life she was in general trade along the East Coast but was abandoned at sea in 1938. Having been recovered and restored she was used in the stone trade from Portland to Greenwich and then became a houseboat in Chelsea. She is now based at St Katharine's Dock in London and available for charter.

Today boat builders and repairers, Spirit Yachts still operate on New Cut East and Fairline Boats now have a test centre along the quay.

In front of the west door is a memorial to one of many shipbuilders associated with St Clement's, Sir Thomas Slade (died 1771). As one of the two joint Surveyors of the Navy, Slade revolutionised naval shipbuilding policy and is most famous for having designed Nelson's flagship, the *Victory*. His wife, Hannah Moore of Nacton, predeceased him and, when he died at Bath, his body was brought back to Ipswich for burial. His grave is lost but the memorial has been erected in his honour.

Although St Clement's is beside the constant traffic of the inner ring road, a certain aura of peace and dignity is nonetheless achieved in its immediate environs. In summer it is surprisingly leafy.

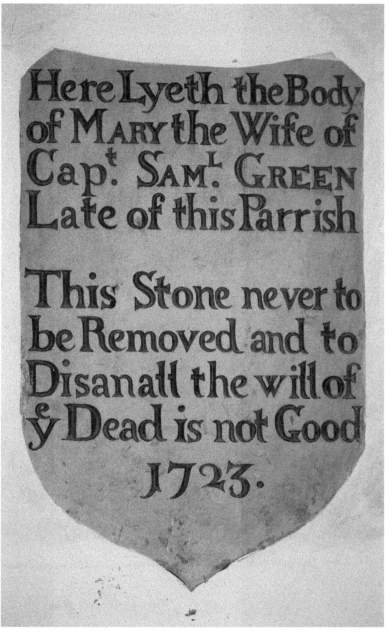

*St Clement's memorial: note Captain Green's use of the Suffolk word 'disanall'.*

The parish was so populous early in the 19th century that Holy Trinity (see above) was built as a Chapel of Ease. Now redundant, St Clement's is under the care of Ipswich Historic Churches Trust but is open on certain days in the summer time and sometimes during the annual Sponsored Bike Ride.

Inside can be found another version of the Arms of Charles II (Walk 2), this time ascribed to 'Mr Bierly' and bearing the two cherubs which are peculiar to Ipswich. Payments were also made to both a painter and iron works so the true instigator of the figures remains mysterious. Whoever it was created a unique town feature. If there was a political point or a contemporary 'in' joke being made it has so far escaped successive town historians.

Here, too, can be seen the wall monument to Captain Samuel Green (died 1723) which warns that 'This stone never to be removed, and to disanall the will of ye dead is not good'.

The word 'disanall' (or 'disannul') is another Suffolk peculiarity and means 'to do away with' or 'to countermand'. As such, Captain Green's bid for immortality preserves a local expression that would otherwise be lost.

**Returning to Grimwade Street along St Clements Church Lane use the island crossing and return to the south side of Fore Street, turning right at Neptune Square.**

Notice the steel sculpture *Trident and Nets* (2000) by Vanessa Parker.

Fore Street is full of things nautical and its eastern end runs approximately parallel to the river. There are 84 listed buildings in Fore Street (2 Grade I, 5 Grade II* and 77 Grade II), more than in any other Ipswich street. Like several other lanes it was one of those that led away from the quayside up to the town marketplaces in mediaeval times.

Daniel Defoe remarked that early in the 1700s Ipswich was a town of very good business and the greatest town in England for large colliers or coal ships employed between Newcastle and London.

He wrote that over a hundred ships' masters lived in the town. They had large families and lived in good houses in the town and several streets were chiefly inhabited by them.

Ipswich was very populous during the winter, wrote Defoe, when many of the ships were laid up. Ships' masters lived 'calm and secure with their families in Ipswich from Michaelmas to Lady Day'. Not only the masters, but their mates, boatswains, carpenters, and all the ship's crew also swelled the population. 'Perhaps a thousand men in the town more than in the summer' wrote Defoe.

Trident and Nets *by Vanessa Parker on Fore Street.*

**Proceed along Fore Street, the Salvation Army building to the right.**

The Café Neptune (on the south side) has a plaque marking the birthplace of Edith Maude Cook (1878–1910), the first woman pilot in Britain and a parachuting pioneer. This intrepid aviator also took some of the earliest hot-air balloon flights, making about 300 ascents before her death aged 31 from injuries sustained in a parachute jump.

Next door is the Old Neptune Inn, a Tudor merchant's house, with shop and warehouses to the rear which extended down to the once-vibrant dock

front. From here merchandise was unshipped, stored and either re-distributed or sold in the town. This is historically one of the most exciting

*Old Neptune Merchant House on Fore Street.*

*Isaac Lord's on Fore Street.*

houses along Fore Street and is a fine example of a hall-house. Its oldest parts are early 15th century, with two top floors and façade added in 1639.

In the 18th century it became an inn and dock labourers received their pay in the bar parlour. Early in the 18th century the same bar was used by Breton onion boys who brought their wares to Ipswich and slept there, stringing their onions around the linen-fold panelling.

The parish of St Clement's was home to the town's merchants who lived alongside their businesses and ships. All the living quarters faced the street while the commercial buildings ran down to the waterside.

Number 80 belonged to Isaac E. Lord, whose name is immortalised on the Waterfront bar complex, Isaac Lord's (Walk 8). The earliest part of the merchant's house dates from the early 1400s, but that abutting Fore Street was erected in 1636.

A little further along, in Salthouse Street, it is possible to see the extended premises of Isaac E. Lord's establishment stretching from Fore Street to the Waterfront.

97 Fore Street (on the north side of the road) is approximately where Thomas Eldred (died 1622) lived. He was an Ipswich merchant and mariner who sailed with Thomas Cavendish on the second English circumnavigation of the globe (1586–88). The Borough Collection has some painted plaster from Eldred's house but the original house was demolished. Those across the street are reminiscent of the style.

**Cross to the north side of Fore Street at the pedestrian crossing in front of The Lord Nelson Inn.**

*The Lord Nelson commemorates the national maritime hero and a one-time high steward of Ipswich.*

The Lord Nelson Inn was at one time called Noah's Ark and known as 'The Ark'. In the 1790s it was one of the designated inns where horses and carriages could be left by those voting in elections. The name was changed in 1805 when Lord Nelson was appointed high sheriff of Ipswich.

It is entirely fitting that a town as thoroughly nautical as Ipswich should have a connection with Viscount Horatio Nelson (1758–1805), Rear Admiral of the Blue Squadron, who in 1798 bought a house off the present Woodbridge Road, known as Roundwood, in which he installed his wife Lady Frances and father, the Revd Edmund Nelson. At his victory at the Battle of the Nile (1798) the town celebrated in style. Lady Nelson attended a grand ball in the town for over 300 guests and the room 'was lighted up with transparencies, and variegated lamps interspersed amongst a variety of evergreens, which had a beautiful effect'.

In 1800 the borough chose Nelson as high steward, but if anyone hoped that he would grace the town with his presence they were disappointed. On the one occasion he did come to visit his wife, the 'hero of the Nile' travelled with Sir William and Lady Hamilton. They arrived in a torrential rainstorm to find that Frances had locked the house up and had gone to London to welcome him home. The party spent the night at the Great White Horse and returned to London the following morning. Shortly afterwards, Lord Nelson and Frances parted and Roundwood was sold off.

*Fore Street Baths just round the corner from The Lord Nelson on the northern stretch of Fore Street.*

Just round the corner behind The Lord Nelson are the Fore Street Baths, erected by the Corporation in 1894. The site and £1,200 towards costs were donated by Felix Cobbold of the brewing Cobbold family whose altruism is in evidence across the town not least in the matter of Christchurch Mansion (Walk 3).

A little further up on the left is a blue plaque to the artist Cor Visser (1903–82). Born in Holland, Cor Visser settled in Ipswich at the end of World War Two, during which he had been official war artist to the Dutch government in exile. He lived for some years on a boat in Ipswich dock, finding inspiration in quayside scenes. In 1962 he made his studio and home at 44 Fore Street.

**Retrace your steps back down Fore Street to Salthouse Street, keeping to the right-hand side of the road, and head westwards onto Key Street until you reach Foundation Street.**

On the corner of Key Street and Foundation Street stands the church of St Mary at the Quay, formerly Stella Maris or Our Lady Star of the Sea, which is sandwiched between two very busy roads.

The present church was constructed between 1450 and 1550 on the site of an older structure. An intriguing aspect of its name is the interchangeable

*St Mary at Quay church stands beside a very busy Key Street.*

spelling of Quay and Key in both church and street for which there seems no rhyme or reason. Its older name was St Mary de Caye (St Mary of the Quay), which would be logical since it stood next to the line of warehouses that once lined the old dock, therefore on or at the 'quay'.

Another theory is that the Danish *kaai* (meaning quayside) is the root and over the years came to be spoken as 'key'. The depiction of a key on the weather vane causes yet more speculation.

St Mary at Quay is referred to in an account of two murderers on the run, who both used its consecrated area as a sanctuary from justice. Being close to the port, it was a popular choice when the 'sanctuary of the church' implied safety from arrest and was recognised as such in English law from the 4th century until 1540 when the Right of Sanctuary was abolished for certain crimes (in 1623, James I effectively abolished it altogether).

The iron closing ring on the 15th-century door was long regarded as an original 'sanctuary ring', grasped by fugitives of the law claiming the right of sanctuary. Having claimed this right, fugitives could not be forcibly removed but were allowed 40 days in which to confess their crimes and take an oath before a coroner to submit to banishment. Thereafter, the fugitive had to dress in a white robe (or sackcloth) and, carrying a wooden cross, must travel to an agreed port aboard the first available ship.

At least two such incidents were recorded at St Mary's: two murderers, John Bryd in 1338 and Nicholas Soweband in 1341, 'fled to the church of St Mary de Caye'.

A similar case of temporary sanctuary occurred in 1339 when John Buckleche, imprisoned in the town gaol for stealing from the Prior of Holy Trinity, escaped and took refuge in All Saints Chapel. John claimed his right to freedom by agreeing to life in exile and serving in the king's army overseas.

Unfortunately, the ring itself is now missing, but you can see where it was once attached.

One famous parishioner of St Mary's was the flamboyant Sir William Sabyn (died 1543), an Ipswich merchant and serjeant-at-arms to Henry VIII, who built the south aisle and whose property adjoined Blackfriars Priory (Walk 4). He enjoyed the colourful pageantry of the Tudor court and is said to have worn gold rings and buttons, crosses and brooches. He was a pioneer sea captain, knowing not only how to sail but also how to fight, and took his own ship, the *Sabyn*, to join in the fray of the early French wars.

William Sabyn was granted Blackfriars at the Dissolution in 1538 and in 1539 was elected representative of the borough in Parliament. He and Henry Tooley worked closely together and used each other's ships on the Bordeaux trade route.

In 1526, Henry Tooley (known as the Great Tooley of Ipswich) of the parish of St Mary at Quay despatched his ship the *Mary Walsingham* to Iceland to bring back salt fish. In the 1520s, Tooley was one of the most active and prosperous merchants in Tudor Ipswich with a factor representing him in the Biscayan ports.

When he died in 1551 he left much of his considerable fortune to founding an almshouse for 10 destitute people. What became known as the Tooley Foundation was later put together with a similar bequest from William Smart (Walk 5). Henry Tooley's table tomb is in the church.

Thomas Pownder, Bailiff of Ipswich and Merchant Adventurer of the same parish, sent out bales of cloth marked with a capital T and two crosses. The ornate Flemish brass of Thomas Pownder and his family (1525) was once in the chancel of St Mary at Quay. It was moved to Christchurch Mansion, where it remained for many years, but it is now in St Peter's Church (see below). It is deemed to be one of the best late mediaeval brasses in England.

St Mary at Quay was one of the churches visited by the Puritan iconoclast William Dowsing in 1643, who recorded in his journal 'I brake down 6 superstitious pictures'.

The church is now in the care of the Churches Conservation Trust and, thanks to help from the Ipswich Historic Churches Trust, St Mary at Quay is open on Thursdays during the summertime.

**Cross over Foundation Street and continue along the north side of what has now become College Street past the old Wolsey Gate (see below) until you come to St Peter's Church.**

*Visitors admire the Ipswich Charter Hangings in St Peter's Church.*

St Peter's Church is one of 12 mediaeval churches to have survived in Ipswich. It appears in the *Domesday Book* (1086) which suggests that there was a much older building here. This earlier structure was closer to the river's edge than the present one (the river banks were wider then) and probably wooden. It is one of the three waterfront churches that served the mariners and merchants of the port.

In 1130 the Augustinian Priory of SS Peter and Paul was founded to the north of the church in grounds of six acres. It was endowed by Henry I and was the first friary to be founded in Ipswich.

The priory was enlarged in 1303 to take account, perhaps, of the demands for hospitality made upon it. Royal patrons expected not only the canons' prayers, and a say in the running of things, but also an unlimited welcome when they or their nominees visited the town. This caused so many problems that it is thought to be the reason why the Order established a second house to the far north of the town where Christchurch Mansion now stands (Walk 3). In 1274 the canons refusal to receive the then sheriff, Walter de Felshanger, led to bitter disputes and 'certain retaliation' by the sheriff. After this and similar incidents the canons petitioned Edward III who promised that the burden of sheltering and feeding itinerant courtiers was no longer binding.

When in 1527 Cardinal Wolsey began preparations for the Cardinal College of St Mary St Peter's was designated the College Chapel. William Brown, the last prior of St Peter and St Paul, surrendered the priory to the cardinal on 6 March 1527. Wolsey's first choice for the site of his new

*A town guide explains the antiquity of the Tournai font in St Peter's Church.*

college had been one near to the Shrine Chapel of Our Lady of Grace (Walk 1). He knew it well, from his childhood and from subsequent pilgrimages. But the Duke of Norfolk advised that it would be cheaper to use St Peter's Priory. The canons were ejected and the parishioners of St Peter's were told to go elsewhere for parochial worship. Two years previously, Wolsey had dissolved over 30 religious houses to pay for the founding and endowing of his colleges at Ipswich and Oxford.

On 15 June 1528 construction was commenced and by September founder pupils were preparing to embark on the educational route planned out for them by their patron. The foundations were said to be both magnificent and sumptuous and were faintly representative of Wolsey's Alma Mata, Magdalen College Oxford.

One of the rituals that Wolsey decreed should be associated with the new college was a procession to the Shrine Chapel to be held annually in September on the Nativity of Our Lady. On that date in 1528, the weather was so atrocious that the dean was not anxious to expose himself, or the finery of his distinguished guests, to the torrential rain and resultant mud. It seems that a practice procession did take place on the Eve of the Nativity but a procession only in the college grounds on the day itself.

Alas, there were no subsequent processions. By September the following year Wolsey's fortunes were already in decline. A few months after his death in 1530 it was learned that the king had decided to dissolve the

*Remaining arch connecting St Peter's to the old priory, looking across to the Novotel.*

*Wolsey's Gate leans precariously towards College Street.*

Cardinal College. The buildings were taken down and the Caen stone removed to London for use in Henry VIII's York House (later Whitehall) in Westminster.

If the church is open there will be someone in attendance who can advise on the salient points in this historic building which is now known as St Peter's by the Waterfront.

On entering the church one of the first things to be seen is the 12th-century Tournai font, made of blue-black marble quarried on the banks of the River Scheldt near Tournai in the Belgian province of Hainault. There are only 10 Tournai marble fonts known to exist in England.

At time of writing, St Peter's is home to The Ipswich Charter Hangings. The eight panels were created for the Millennium and to celebrate 800 years since the granting of King John's Charter in 1200.

A guide to St Peter's is available inside the church.

## Return to College Street.

A remnant of the college is the famous Wolsey Gate, which can be seen a short way along College Street to the left. The red-brick gateway that led to the river now leans precariously over the pavement beside non-stop traffic:

it suffers badly from years of exposure to car exhaust fumes and is all that is left of Wolsey's college.

An arch on the north side of the church is part of a wall that probably once connected it to the priory.

To reach the Waterfront use the pedestrian crossing in front of the church and follow Bridge Street towards Stoke Bridge.

**To return to the UCS turn left along the Waterfront (Walk 8).**

For a longer walk that is rewarded by splendid views of the Waterfront and river activity, carry on past the UCS and the Neptune Marina gates, and follow Orwell Quay along New Cut. Here is the departure point for the *Orwell Lady* river cruises.

On the left is the £22 million James Hehir Building, opened in March 2011. It is UCS's newest addition and will house specialist science laboratories and a new student union bar.

It is named in memory of James Hehir, the Ipswich Borough Council chief executive who championed UCS and the Waterfront development. During the opening ceremony a time capsule was buried by UCS Provost Professor Mike Saks. It contains a personal message from the provost, original blueprints, photographs and cards from students.

*The James Hehir building on Orwell Quay.*

*Details of the* Orwell Lady *river cruises are available at the TIC or from their website.*

A few yards along is a frieze that marks the departure of adventurers and emigrants to the New World (Walk 5). *Beyond the Horizon* by Dan Savage (2007) is a 12m-long vitreous enamel piece on glass commemorating the 400 years since the founding of Jamestown, Virginia (USA) in 1607.

From here there are incomparable views of the marinas and a chance to watch the comings and going on the water. On the opposite side stand Spirit Yachts and Fairline yacht builders, keeping alive the age-old tradition of Ipswich boat building.

*View back to the Ipswich Waterfront from Orwell Quay.*

# WALK 8

## THE WATERFRONT

Walk 8 begins at UCS and finishes at Stoke Bridge, taking in:
*University Campus Suffolk (UCS) – Neptune Quay – Wherry Lane – Salthouse Street – Isaac Lord's – Common Quay – Old Custom House – Albion Quay – St Peter's Dock – Stoke Bridge – Stoke Street – New Cut – Haven Marina*

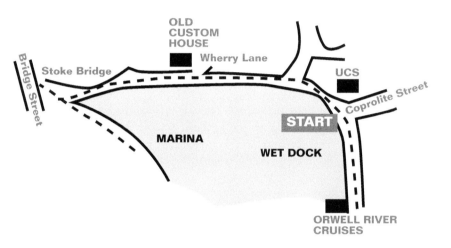

This walk is a leisurely stroll – almost traffic-free – along the Waterfront where there are numerous cafés and restaurants strung along the quays. If arriving by car, follow signs to Waterfront Car Park or, if by bus, see Town Transport.

The port of Ipswich developed along a bend in the River Orwell and has been a centre for national and international trade since at least the late 6th century. The port and town though always connected grew independently, which explains why the two still today have separate characters. Indeed, prior to the Reformation the annual Procession of the Host, organised by the Corpus Christi Merchants Guild, was led on alternate years by the Priors of St Peter's (to represent the waterfront to the south) and those of Christchurch (for the town to the north).

During the reign of Edward III (1327–77) Ipswich was one of the richest and most important ports in the country. Indeed, the king was frequently in these parts, especially during 1338 when he began assembling his fleets in the Orwell Estuary prior to raising an expeditionary force at the start of what became The Hundred Years War with France. Those in the town were, however, ambivalent towards the king as he had temporarily granted many of their privileges to Harwich, infringing their rights to the waters of the 'port of Orwell' and tolls deriving from commercial shipping. The town burgesses remonstrated with the king who eventually revoked his charter to Harwich, restoring the borough's entitlements to the import duties levied on goods going through the port of Ipswich.

At this time large numbers of Welsh longbow archers arrived in the town and in 1340 the king's fleet of 200 sailing warships anchored in the estuary. The town authorities were constantly worried about the stability of their port and were not entirely enamoured of the unprecedented influx. Considerable demands were made on town resources for victualling and billeting the gathering troops and royal retinue. Many were pleased to see the back of Edward III's fleet when he finally set sail for France. In the event the English routed the French at the Battle of Sluys, thereafter dominating the English Channel and preventing French invasions.

Relations between Ipswich and the king deteriorated somewhat a few years later when Edward placed the town temporarily under the control of his sheriff after a mob of sailors stormed the court house and held a daring mock trial of the king's own judge of assizes.

Edward III returned to the Orwell in 1346 and again amassed a large fleet, this time reputed to be 300 warships, which later gained victory at the Battle of Crecy. Waging war was expensive, not only in monetary terms but in regard to men and ships. King Edward was one of those monarchs forced to pardon those merchants engaged in piracy where he needed ships and men for war. Among those from Ipswich who were pardoned was William Malyn and his son, also William.

The reference to the 'port of Orwell' in the dispute of 1340 has, over the years, given rise to speculation that there was once a town called Orwell somewhere close to Ipswich, or that Ipswich itself was once called Orwell. No firm conclusions have yet been drawn.

The origin of the name Orwell turns up in *Hollinshed's Chronicles* (1580) when the river is apparently called the Ure 'at the mouth whereof is a marvellous deep and large pit some mariners say they could never find the bottom of, and therefore calling it a well'. The Ure-well thereafter became Orwell.

After centuries of shipping, trade ebbed away in the 18th century when the Orwell began to silt up. Only small vessels could make it to the quays and the larger ones unloaded on to lighters below Downham Reach. By the 1740s there were continual complaints from ship owners about the state of the quays and the restrictions caused by the rise and fall of the tide. Low tide left ships sitting idly on the mud and at times tipping dangerously and damaging the wharves. It was obvious that unless something was done, the port of Ipswich would cease to function.

In 1805 the Corporation had responsibility for administering the port but those who used its services considered there was 'neglectful indifference' to its poor state. Accordingly, 72 local men formed themselves into a body known as the River Commissioners and obtained an Act of Parliament to empower them to carry out the 'deepening, widening, cleansing, altering and otherwise improving' the river between Stoke Bridge and Levington Creek. Local ship owners, though, wanted more than just improvements and began pressing for a Wet Dock with locks which would allow ships into the dock without letting the water out so that the vessels inside were protected from the fluctuations in tide levels.

When the Wet Dock was opened in 1842 it was a pioneering, ambitious and very grand project. It contained a total floating area of 33 acres and had taken four years to build. At high tide on 6 September 1843, the lock gates were closed and thus Ipswich harbour became the largest wet dock in Great Britain. It was completed just in time for the town to begin taking full advantage of the upcoming Victorian prosperity which once again saw the docks become important in the commercial life of Ipswich.

*The modern shape of the Wet Dock built in a bend in the Orwell river.*

*The Neptune Marina has berths for 250 boats.*

In 1881 a larger lock was opened and in 1904 almost 800ft of new quay was built.

In the 1930s and 40s millions of tons of shipping passed through the port either as imports or exports. Phosphate and lime came from Casablanca, wheat and timber from Canada and Philadelphia.

During World War Two part of the dock was used as a refitting and repairing base for sloops, mine-sweepers and trawlers. The Admiralty occupied part of Cliff Quay as a trawler base.

After the heyday of the Thames sailing barges, the Wet Dock's fortunes declined as larger vessels could not access it and the ships had to load and unload further down stream (as they do today). By the 1970s there was little commercial traffic, but in the early 1990s post-industrial development of the Waterfront began.

Since then it has been in a state of constant change and looks set to continue that way for some years, although the recession has slowed progress. The whole nature of its reason to exist is moving from industrial and agricultural shipping to housing, leisure and education. Gone are the Victorian warehouses associated with corn and coal: instead it is the imposing UCS building, cafés and restaurants which are strung along the quays in between apartment buildings and the Salthouse Hotel.

In the Wet Dock and Haven Marina modern yachts and power boats replace the 19th-century sailing barges, except for charter vessels like the sailing barge *Victor* which moor alongside Common Quay (see below).

*UCS in the early morning light.*

Passing along Neptune Quay one of the first modern buildings on the Waterfront is that of University Campus Suffolk, which has a distinctive curved structure and multi-coloured windows. UCS was created in 2007 (in collaboration with the University of East Anglia and the University of Essex) and opened in September 2008. It now has over 3,600 students with plans to grow to 7,500 by 2014. UCS's newest addition is the James Hehir Building, which was opened in 2011 (Walk 7).

*UCS is part of the reflective town architecture.*

*View from UCS onto Fore Street.*

The Salthouse Hotel is also on Neptune Quay and, like Coprolite Street (Walk 7), is a reminder of the industries plied here, in particular the important salt trade. The hotel takes its name from Salthouse Street which in turn derives from the Salt Office that was set up to administer the huge quantities of this commodity brought into the port from the Tyne in the early 1700s. Salt, which also came from the Cheshire salt mines, was used for cattle licks and by the tanners in the preservation of hides.

*The UCS building is noted for its innovative coloured windows.*

*Saturday afternoon at Isaac Lord's on the Waterfront.*

In the 1930s corn and coal was traded from the quays in front of the Isaac Lord Complex which takes it name from Isaac Lord, a local businessman who bought the property from the Cobbold brewing family in 1900. Some of the buildings date from early 15th century and others to the late 18th, reflecting commercial and industrial use over many centuries.

*'Nogging' brickwork on Isaac Lord building, visible from Wherry Lane.*

*Isaac Lord's and the Salthouse Hotel on the Waterfront.*

Within the complex lies the Sale Room, where the all-important medieval wool and fabric trading took place and dates from the time when Ipswich was one of only four authorised wool centres in East Anglia. The Sale Room was used in connection with the exportation of wool and wholesale trading of imported goods. Finished cloth from the surrounding Suffolk weaving villages was also gathered here for sale and then shipped to Europe and beyond.

During the time that it was owned by the Cobbolds some of the buildings were used as a maltings. The kiln in which the malt was dried was converted into a public house in 1984.

The Machinery Room houses machines used in the brewing industry and one of the mill pieces used to roll oats to feed horses at the Tolly Cobbold Brewery is still in working order. The Machinery Room is unique to Suffolk and some of the parts still operable date back to the 18th century.

Notice the dipped contour of the Courtyard Bar which shows where the 'cut' was that connected the warehouses to the river, originally much deeper and filled with water.

The Viking Mariners is on the corner of Wherry Lane. They organise sailing days and corporate hospitality on the River Orwell. It also has offices for Boat Sales UK (a division of Nautco Limited) and a marine-related clothing outlet, Promenade.

For such a small thoroughfare Wherry Lane is always busy, especially now with all the renewed activity on the Waterfront. The John Russell Art Gallery is worth a look. The gallery proprietor is Anthony 'Tony' Coe, a man of many talents who toured the world as a guitarist with some of the best-known names in entertainment, including The Who and Jimi Hendrix. In the 1960s he played with the American 'soul shouter' Geno Washington and the Ram Jam Band.

Notice the Sarsen stones placed along the wall base to protect the building from horses and carriages as they passed along the narrow lane.

The connecting buildings between Isaac Lord's (Walk 7) and the Waterfront can be seen from the Salthouse Street end of Wherry Lane. The exposed 'nogging' brickwork was used to fill in the spaces between the studs and frames and is set on the diagonal, making a distinctive pattern.

Back on the Waterfront, Waterfront House was for many years the headquarters of the Contship Containers shipping company. At the time it was converted into offices the work was seen as a radical renovation project. Known as Home Warehouse, the present structure is fashioned out of a 19th century disused grain warehouse retaining the internal loading bins and hoppers. It is now solicitors' offices.

The historic Grade II-listed Old Custom House was built in 1844–45 from red-and-white brick and stone, a combination of materials that gives it a special place in architectural history. It overlooks the Wet Dock and now houses the offices of the Ipswich Port Authority with a conference centre on the ground floor. There was previously an older custom house on the same site.

The blue doors leading straight off the quay were once used to take prisoners into the police station at the back of the custom house. Cells that were part of the police station can still be seen inside the building.

There is no public access to the Old Custom House, but if the gates are open there are good photo opportunities from the parapets at the top of the steps.

Those stylish colonnades further along on the dockside are the remains of what were once warehouses and mills built as part of the Wet Dock project. Parts of the old Victorian buildings remain awaiting completion of redevelopment.

The Thames sailing barge, *Victor*, is often moored opposite the Old Custom House alongside the Common Quay. She was built in Ipswich in 1895 for work in the linseed oil trade. Until World War Two the *Victor* collected linseed from farms around the East Coast, took it to a mill at Colchester, and continued to London with the oil in barrels.

During the war she loaded munitions out of Chatham dock and miraculously survived a bomb that completely destroyed a lighter lying nearby.

*UCS across the deck of SB* Victor.

She was eventually restored and refitted to carry passengers for summer leisure cruises. In winter the *Victor* also offers regular bird-watching cruises on the rivers Orwell and Stour.

In the early years of the 20th century sailing barges were a common sight up and down the coast and at one time the Wet Dock would have been full to bursting as they provided the commercial lifeblood of the county. The arrival of the railways in 1846 posed a challenge to sea traffic but the dock continued to prosper nevertheless.

*SB* Victor *in front of the Old Custom House (Contship building to the right)*

Two other sailing barges can also be seen beside Common Quay during the summer, *Thistle* and *Hydrogen*, both of which operate charter trips. *Thistle* was built in the Clyde in 1895, making her, along with the *Victor*, contemporary with the heyday of the Wet Dock. The presence of the barges, with their tower masts and brown sails, adds a certain romance and enchantment to the quaysides, a picturesque reminder of the great days of sail.

The largest sailing ships to have used the port were the merchant vessels known as 'windjammers', which took part in the famous Grain Races from Australia of the inter-war years. They operated from the 1870s until the 1930s, when steamships began to outpace them. One big square rigger came every year, until 1939, with Australian wheat for the Ipswich flour mills. The Orwell was not then dredged as deeply as it is today, so the grain ships were towed up to Butterman's Bay. The cargo was taken off by sailing barges which then brought it up to the mills in the Wet Dock. Once the square riggers were high enough in the water they proceeded to Cliff Quay and the lower Wet Dock, a shorter distance away where the remainder was again transferred to barges and taken to the dock head quays.

Among the best known ships to come here was the *Melbourne* and the four-masted barque *Herzogin Cecilie*, an archetypal 'windjammer' built in 1902. In April 1936, the *Herzogin Cecilie* was making for Ipswich in dense fog when she grounded off the Devon coast. She had travelled from Australia to Falmouth in only 86 days, the second-fastest time ever, but it was to be her last voyage. Parts of the cargo were unloaded (Pauls of Ipswich sent their barges

*The Window Museum on the Waterfront, just before the colonnades.*

down to fetch what they could) but soon afterwards the pounding waves broke her apart. The remains of the ship still lie on the sea bed.

Look down the alley – just before the Jerwood Dance House (on the ground floor of The Mill) – at the exhibition in the Window Museum on Albion Quay curated by the Ipswich Maritime Trust. It is claimed to be England's only Window Museum. The Trust was set up in 1982 with the declared aim of educating the people of Suffolk 'in all matters maritime'.

Jerwood Dance House, home to the region's leading dance organisation, DanceEast, has three dance studios, a 200-seat flexible space studio theatre, fitness and pilates suite, and café. It is on the ground floor of the 23-storey 'landmark' building, The Mill, which is one of East Anglia's tallest buildings.

A custom-built peregrine nest box is set within the parapet of The Mill, 230ft above the Waterfront. It is part of the second phase in the Suffolk Ornithologists' Group's plan to entice wild falcons back to Suffolk after an absence of more than 200 years. A peregrine box sited 140ft up on the Orwell Bridge has met with considerable success and it is hoped that a second pair of birds will make full use of what has become known as the peregrine 'penthouse' suite.

**Leaving the Waterfront with The Mill to the right (on St Peter's Dock), Stoke Bridge is straight ahead.**

On Stoke Bridge (sometimes known as St Peter's Bridge) is a spherical red-and-white Trinity House buoy. It is an old Middle Ground Mark of the type

*The Mill (centre) towers over the Waterfront and can be seen from the town.*

discontinued in 1977 and is purely a civic ornamentation. It is no longer a navigational aid and has no significance to the river or any craft using the New Cut.

Hereabouts is known as the Stoke Crossing, referred to locally as 'Over Stoke'. In 970 King Edgar granted the whole of Stoke parish to the monks of Ely and the grant itself contains the early word for Ipswich, *Gipeswic*, for the first time.

Stoke is the Saxon word for 'stockade' and the south bank parish pre-dates the Saxon era when it was a fortified hill protected by water and marshes.

The Stoke Crossing marks the earliest river crossing between the north and south banks. Here the river was forded for the first time and a bridge is known to have existed as early as AD970 to serve mediaeval trade and communication routes. The river was much broader in early times, stretching almost from St Peter's Church (Walk 7) to the Old Bell Inn (see below). The quays would have been nothing more sophisticated than wooden stakes driven into the mud and woven with laths or withies. Unlike many such places that were abandoned, the *Gipeswic* quays were repeatedly extended and embanked. Successive revetments were built out into the river so that ships could moor alongside.

Underneath the Novotel Hotel (on the north side of the roundabout) was discovered evidence for the earliest days of Ipswich. Wells found there were lined with barrels from Germany, carbon-dated to the sixth century, along with early Frankish pottery.

Numerous lanes would have led away from this early crossing towards the town markets and on one or other bank there would have been a gatekeeper of sorts with authority to levy taxes or tolls in accordance with the prevailing market regulations. A map of Ipswich dated 1539 clearly shows a gatehouse on both the north and south banks of the Stoke bridge, which would have served as a town gate. A building of some kind was still there in 1674, as shown on the first detailed large-scale map of the town by John Ogilby.

The present bridge was constructed in 1924–25 and replaced an iron one built by Ransome & Son in 1819 after the old stone bridge was destroyed by a flood in 1818. An area of timber-framed houses was demolished to make way for the most recent construction.

There was a watermill at Stoke Bridge where the Riot Act was once read. Driven to desperation by the scarcity and high prices of food in 1800, a mob of townsmen stormed the mill. The cavalry was summoned from the town barracks and, after the reading of the Riot Act, the townsmen were turned back and order restored.

Looking from the bridge down towards the Waterfront (the Wet Dock), the River Orwell (called New Cut at that point) is seen on the right, flowing under the bridge into the estuary and eventually out to sea. New Cut was constructed in 1840 to direct the river water away from the newly-built Wet Dock.

*Bridge over the Wet Dock lock entrance swinging across.*

*A mixture of the old and new on Ipswich Waterfront.*

From the bridge (which should be bridges, as there are two, side by side) the church tower and roof of St Mary at Stoke is seen. It is the only mediaeval church on the south side of the river.

On the far bank of the river (to the right) is the old Felaw Maltings building, which is considered to be a good example of 19th-century industrial architecture. The buildings are now converted to offices.

Over the bridge on the corner of Stoke Street stands the late 16th-century Old Bell Inn 'reputably the oldest pub in Ipswich'. At time of writing it is closed for business, and plans for its future are being considered. There are two interesting carvings on a corner post, a bell and a sea creature, that would reward a short walk across the bridge. Although strictly speaking in St Peter's parish, it has traditionally been considered a Stoke pub. Once considerably larger, it was a regular haunt for carriers and farmers who passed along Bell Lane in and out of the town. In the 18th century it was famous for the cock fights held in the stable yard which were advertised regularly in the *Ipswich Journal*.

It was formerly thought that the inn took its name from a nearby bell foundry, but there are no records of, or evidence for, such a foundry having operated in that part of the town. 'Bell' was a familiar and common appellation for an inn, especially if they were within the sound of the bells of a church, in this case St Mary at Stoke. There was, however, a foundry in Bury St Edmunds and a bell made there by the noted bell maker Stephan Toni (in 1579) can be seen at Christchurch Mansion (Walk 3).

In 1763, however, a Noah Bloomfield gave notice in the *Ipswich Journal* that he had taken the Ram Inn (on the Common Key) and intended to carry on the 'bell foundry' at the home of the late William Rayment where 'brasses of all sorts are cast to perfection'. Whether or not this has anything to do with a possible bell foundry next to the Old Bell Inn, however, is open to discussion.

The bell carving is not as old as the sea creature below and was carved in the 19th century by an eminent Ipswich wood carver, Mr Ringham. The sea creature (or sea horse), looking more feline than equine, is likely to date from the 15th century and might have inspired the inn's previous name, The Sea Horse.

A board on the outside wall of the inn shows a bell of the parish of St Mary le Bow – the Number 12 Curfew Bell – that was destroyed by fire in 1334. This has given rise to thoughts that the Curfew Bell could have been struck in Ipswich, which is unlikely. However, the picture on the sign is a straight copy (in every detail) of the Whitechapel foundry postcard of the present Bow tenor (at St Mary-le-Bow) and has the same inscription. It is a popular illustration for public houses named The Bell.

*Ipswich Haven Marina gives another perspective on the Waterfront.*

*The curious cat-like carving on the Old Bell Inn, 'Over Stoke'.*

There are also echoes of the Bow Bells in the cat-like sea creature carved on the inn's corner post. Could it have something to do with Sir Richard Whittington, real life model for the pantomime character, 'Dick Whittington' (Walk 6) who was recalled to London by the sound of Bow Bells? Perhaps the carving was inspired by the Ipswich Cat ships, so named for the style of rig, that sailed to and from the port in the 13th century, one of which appears on the Corporation seal (now called the Borough seal) of 1200.

The Old Bell Inn was listed Grade II in 1951.

**For a longer walk and to explore the east side of New Cut and Haven Marina, return to Jerwood Dance House (The Mill) and follow the footpath signs to Ipswich Haven Marina round to the right and then left along the fencing. From here are obtained views across the Wet Dock to the Old Custom House and across the Waterfront to UCS.**

Besides the Burton Waters Chandlery, there is a restaurant and facilities for visiting yachtsmen.

**Otherwise, retrace steps to UCS Car Park or bus stop.**

To reach the town centre from Stoke Bridge cross College Street then head north, with St Peter's Church to the right. Follow St Peter's Street to the junction with Silent Street and turn right. At the top of Silent Street cross the Old Cattle Market onto St Stephen's Lane, where is found the Tourist Information Centre.

# USEFUL INFORMATION AND CONTACTS

**Ipswich Tourist Information Centre (TIC)**
St Stephen's Church
St Stephen's Lane
Ipswich, IP1 1DP
01473 432018
**www.visit-ipswich.com**
Open: Monday to Saturday 9am–5pm.

**Ipswich Borough Council**
Grafton House
15–17 Russell Road
Ipswich, IP1 2DE
01473 432000
**www.ipswich.gov.uk**

**Suffolk County Council**
Endeavour House
Russell Road
Ipswich, IP1 2BX
01473 583000
**www.suffolk.gov.uk**

**University Campus Suffolk (UCS)**
Ipswich Campus
Waterfront Building
Neptune Quay
Ipswich, IP4 1QJ
01473 338000
**www.ucs.ac.uk**

**UCS at Suffolk New College**
Rope Walk
Ipswich, IP4 1LT
**www.ucs.ac.uk**

## Ipswich Museum

High Street
Ipswich, IP1 3QH
01473 433558
**www.ipswich.gov.uk**

## Ipswich Transport Museum

Old Trolleybus Depot
Cobham Road
Ipswich, IP3 9JD
01473 715666
**www.ipswichtransportmuseum.co.uk**
The ITM has the largest collection of transport items in Britain devoted to just one town (including Ransomes of Ipswich).

## Ipswich Town Football Club

Portman Road
Ipswich, IP1 2DA
**www.itfc.co.uk**

## Ipswich Town Supporters' Club

**www.itfcsupporters.co.uk**

## Neptune Marina

Neptune Quay
Ipswich, IP4 1AX
01473 215204
**www.neptune-marine.com**

## Ipswich Haven Marina

Tovells Wharf
New Cut East
Ipswich, IP3 OEA
01473 236644
**www.isuffolk.co.uk**
270-berth in Wet Dock
Opened in 2000.

## Burton Waters Chandlery
Ipswich Haven Marina
New Cut East
Ipswich, IP3 0EA
01473 232469
**www.burtonwaters.co.uk**

## Orwell River Cruises
Tourist Information Office
St Stephen's Lane
Ipswich, IP1 1DP
01473 258070
**www.orwellrivercruises.com**
Day Cruises: Ipswich to Harwich Harbour (May–September) and Ipswich to
Pin Mill (July–August).

## Ipswich Waterfront Action Partnership Group
20 Back Hamlet
Ipswich, IP3 8AJ
0773 199669
**jay@waterfrontaction.co.uk**

For details of the annual Ipswich Maritime Festival
**www.waterfrontaction.co.uk/ipswichmaritimefestival**

## Suffolk Record Office
Gatacre Road
Ipswich, IP1 2LQ
Searchroom: 01473 584541
Email: **ipswich.ro@suffolk.gov.uk**
**www.suffolk.gov.uk/LeisureAndCulture/**

## Ipswich Arts Festival (Ip-art)
(Annual Summer Festival)
Ipswich Arts and Entertainment Box Office
01473 433100
**www.ip-art.com**

## Ipswich Arts Association
Umbrella organisation for Ipswich and district arts scene with on-line *images*
magazine and arts calendar.
**www.ipswich-arts.org.uk**

## New Wolsey Theatre
Civic Drive
Ipswich, IP1 2AS
01473 295500
**www.wolseytheatre.co.uk**
Annual Pulse Fringe Festival of drama and music in venues across town, organised by New Wolsey Theatre.

## Ipswich Historic Churches Trust
**www.ipswich.gov.uk**
Established 1979, the Trust now cares for the churches of St Lawrence, St Peter, St Clement, St Stephen and St Nicholas.

## The Ipswich Society
28 Balliol Close
Woodbridge, Suffolk, IP12 4EQ
**www.ipswichsociety.org**
A PDF version of the current Blue Plaques leaflet is available from the society website.

## BBC Radio Suffolk
Broadcasting House
St Matthew's Street
Ipswich, IP1 3EP
01473 212121
**www.bbc.co.uk/suffolk**

## *Ipswich Evening Star*
Archant Suffolk
Press House
Lower Brook Street
Ipswich, IP4 1AN
01473 230023
**www.eveningstar.co.uk**
Daily evening newspaper for Ipswich.

## *East Anglian Daily Times*
Archant Suffolk
Press House
Lower Brook Street
Ipswich, IP4 1AN
01473 230023
**www.eadt.co.uk**
Monday–Saturday county-wide newspaper (and North Essex).

### Ipswich Angle

Grafton House
Russell Road
Ipswich, IP1 2DE
01473 432031
**www.ipswich-angle.com**
**www.ipswich.gov.uk**
Free Ipswich Borough Council newspaper containing news, views, culture, sport and entertainment in Ipswich: available at public venues in the town with online information about town attractions, restaurants, etc. downloadable as a PDF.

### River Gipping Trust Limited

Church Cottage
Capel St Mary
Ipswich, IP9 2EL
**www.rivergippingtrust.org.uk**

### Gipping Valley River Path

Stowmarket to Ipswich River Path following the old Gipping Navigation towpath (Walk 6)
**www.suffolk.gov.uk/Environment/Country Walks**
**www.britishwalks.org**

ND - #0308 - 270225 - C0 - 210/136/12 - PB - 9781780913223 - Gloss Lamination